Euripides' *Medea*

Euripides' *Medea*

Translated
with an Introduction
and Notes

A.J. Podlecki

Focus Classical Library
Focus Publishing/R. Pullins Company
PO Box 369
Newburyport MA 01950

Medea
© 1989 by A.J. Podlecki

Focus Publishing/R. Pullins Company
PO Box 369
Newburyport, MA 01950
www.pullins.com

Cover Photo: Story, William Wetmore (1819-1895). *Medea.* 1865; this version, 1868. Marble, 82¼x26¾x27½ in. (208.9x67.9x69.9 cm). Detail. Location: The Metropolitan Museum of Art, New York, NY, U.S.A. Gift of Henry Chauncey, 1894. (94.8a-d). Photograph by Jerry L. Thompson. Copyright © The Metropolitan Museum of Art/Art Resource, NY

Back cover image © istockphoto / aaM Photography Ltd.

ISBN: 978-0-941051-10-1

2005 Revised Printing

Printed in the United States of America

18 17 16 15 14 13 12 11 10 9

1113TS

Contents

Helios
|
Aites
|
Hecate
|
Medea — Jason
|
Medeios

Introduction

The Mythical Background

It is clear from scattered references in our sources that Medea and her various adventures belong to the earliest stratum of Greek myth. The episodes that are most familiar to the modern reader are those recounted or alluded to in Euripides' play, in a short passage in Pindar's Fourth Pythian Ode, and in an epic poem which survives, *The Adventures of the Argonauts (Argonautica),* by the Hellenistic writer Apollonius of Rhodes. But there were other stories, some perhaps of greater currency in ancient Greece than the ones best known to us. The version we consider as standard makes of Medea a priestess (or even a daughter) of the moon-goddess Hecate, and herself a witch, daughter of Aietes, who was the brother of Circe, both of them children of Helios the Sun-god. The locus of this magical family was Colchis, on the remote eastern shore of Pontus, "The Sea," known to the Greeks also as "Euxine" ("Hospitable," a title of hope) and to the modern traveler as the Black Sea. But another series of stories placed Medea firmly (if mythically) in the genealogy of Corinth's ruling family. According to this account, which had behind it the authority of the Corinthian poet Eumelus (probably somewhat earlier than Homer, and so before 700 B.C.), Helios gave his son Aietes Corinth—then known as Ephyra—as part of his domain. When Aietes in answer to an oracle went off to Colchis, the kingship passed to his brother Aloeus and then to some of his descendants who, however, because of certain difficulties they got into, made the people of Ephyra-Corinth regret that Aietes had given up the kingship. So they summoned Aietes' daughter Medea from where she was living, Iolkos in Thessaly, and she became their queen; her husband Jason followed her and

1

they ruled jointly. Wishing to make their children immortal (this was apparently because of a false promise by Hera), as each was born Medea "hid" them (that is, buried them alive) in Hera's sanctuary at Corinth, but when Jason learned what she was doing he, quite naturally, disapproved and returned to Iolkos, so Medea, too, left Corinth and turned the kingdom over to Sisyphus (see note on v. 405 below; in a variant, known to Pindar, she married Sisyphus and presumably ruled Corinth with him). Although there are points of contact with at least one event in Euripides' play, her murder of her children, this is a very different and somewhat more respectable series of adventures than the better-known version.

She comes into the story of the Argonauts ("Sailors on the ship *Argo*") when the exploits of these Dark Age buccaneers are already well under way. Homer knew the tale, even though he chose not to tell it, simply referring to it in several places in an offhand way (he refers to the *Argo* as "the sea-faring ship which everyone is concerned with," indicating perhaps that he felt enough poetic accounts were already in circulation). Jason, he says, was the only sailor to escape shipwreck on the "Wandering Rocks" (see note on v. 2, "Clashing Rocks"), because he was helped by the goddess Hera, who loved him. Elsewhere Homer records Thessalian Iolkos as the kingdom of Pelias, half-brother of Aison, who was Jason's father. And of course the witch Circe, daughter of Helios and sister of Aietes, figures prominently in the story of Odysseus' wanderings.

If Homer never mentions Medea by name she does find a place, albeit a small one, in Hesiod's *Theogony*, which gives a brief account of the "labors" imposed by Pelias on his nephew, Jason. During his journeys, we learn, Jason met Medea and brought the "flashing-eyed maiden" back to Iolkos with him as his wife; they had a son, Medeios (elsewhere called Medos), whom the centaur Chiron raised. It is assumed that Medea figured in the genealogical poetry, now lost, which was current at Hesiod's time and later, and some details are specifically assigned to the non-extant *Naupactica*, "Tales about Naupactus." As we shall see, one of her tricks was narrated in the *Nostoi*, "Returns," which was part of the so-called epic "Cycle" intended to fill out the Trojan tales told by Homer. Medea was best known, however, for the help she rendered to Jason in his quest of the Golden Fleece, a tale alluded to by the early elegiac poet Mimnermus in a work that does not survive, and it is to this segment of Medea's story that we must now turn.

Jason's father Aison had been deprived of his kingdom, Iolkos, through the treachery of Aison's half-brother, Pelias. Pelias, however, had received an oracular prophecy that he would have to surrender the kingship to a legitimate claimant known only as "the half-shod man." When Aison's son, Jason, appeared, meeting this specification, Pelias tried to delay the transfer of authority by sending Jason to fulfill a seemingly impossible labor, retrieval of a golden ram's fleece from a distant corner of the world, Colchis. (According to the early prose-writer Pherecydes, Pelias had incurred the anger of the goddess Hera, who prompted Jason to ask to have this "impossible" task performed because she knew full well that in the event Jason would manage to accomplish it with the aid of the sorceress Medea, who would return with Jason and become the ultimate instrument of Pelias' death.) Jason rigged the ship *Argo* (meaning "Swift" or "Gleaming") made from timber cut on Mt. Pelion (cf. vv. 3-4 below), and gathered a crew of renowned ship-mates, including Heracles. His travels, which some have interpreted as reflecting the Greeks' increasing knowledge of faraway places as a result of the opening up of seafaring trade in the 8th century, took him ultimately to Colchis, land of dragons, where King Aietes agreed to surrender the fleece if Jason performed another labor, yoking a pair of fire-breathing bulls (see vv. 478-9), driving a straight furrow, sowing some dragon's teeth given him by Aietes, and mastering the armed warriors, or "Sown Men," who would spring up from the soil to oppose him. At this point, Aietes' daughter Medea enters Jason's story. In several accounts she falls under the spell of Jason's manly charms; more specifically, the goddess Aphrodite worked upon Medea's heart, possibly also at the prompting of Hera, who had taken a liking to Jason, as we saw. Medea knew that her father had no intention of honoring his promise to Jason: she was torn between her love for the newcomer and a sense of filial piety and family obligation. She contemplated suicide but after a great deal of inner turmoil decided to yield to her passion. She gave Jason a magic unguent which made him impervious to the bulls' fiery breath and a "stone of discord" which he threw among the Sown Men that sprang up from the dragon's teeth, who fought each other to the death but left Jason alone. When he was at last ready to face the dragon who guarded the Golden Fleece, Medea concocted an emulsion made by soaking a branch of juniper, whose fumes tranquilized the dragon long enough for Jason to retrieve the fleece and head for his ship.

So far, Medea's magic has appeared in a relatively benign form. But when her father Aietes set out in pursuit of the couple Medea, foreseeing this eventuality, produced the severed limbs of her brother Apsyrtos, whom she had previously murdered (see v. 1334 and elsewhere in the play), and proceeded to scatter them in the *Argo's* wake, knowing that her father's religious scruples would oblige him to delay the pursuit in order to collect the limbs for burial. (Another account had Apsyrtos pursue Medea and Jason up the Danube as far as an island in the Adriatic [!] where, with Medea's help, Jason was able to decoy him and kill him.) Various embellishments were recounted concerning the latter part of the return trip: they turned up at the island of Medea's aunt, Circe, who originally agreed to purify the couple but, when she learned the horrendous nature of their crime, drove them away; or they landed in Alcinous' kingdom of Phaeacia, where they first consummated their marriage in a grotto, and Alcinous agreed to give them protection. After a detour to Crete, where Medea again helped Jason, this time to overpower Minos' bronze robot, Talos, the couple returned to Iolkos so that Jason could take up his kingdom, as his uncle had agreed. When Pelias renèged on his promise and refused to surrender power to Jason, Medea devised a particularly hideous revenge. She gave an advance demonstration of her magic powers, rejuvenating a ram by immersing it in a boiling cauldron (according to a passage from the Cyclic epic *Nostoi*, mentioned above, quoted in an ancient Plot Summary to *Medea* [see page 79], at some point in their life together she performed a similar rejuvenation on Jason's father, Aison). She then persuaded Pelias' daughters that, if they cut up their father and followed the recipe, the effect would be the same. In fact, this simply resulted in Pelias' death; the celebration of his funeral games, with gods and heroes in attendance, was a favorite theme in archaic Greek poetry and art. Pelias' son Acastus (brother of Alcestis who, however, had not participated in the boiling) exiled his sisters for their guilty foolishness, as well as Jason and Medea.

The couple appeared at Corinth and their stay there followed the outlines of Euripides' plot: Jason's renunciation of Medea and "political" alliance with the princess, variously named Glauke or Creusa in the sources (she is not given a name in the play), and Medea's revenge. When Euripides came to devise his dénouement, one tradition he might have followed was that Medea, after killing King Creon and his daughter (who, in order to escape the ravages of Medea's poisons, threw herself into a fountain named afterwards "Glauke" to commemorate the deed) fled to Athens, leaving her sons behind at an altar of Hera and expecting that their father would save them from the reprisals of the king's relatives. This Jason did not, or could not, do, and the children were slain by the Corinthians who, to cover up their crime, put about the rumor that their mother had killed them. (As we have seen there was another early variant: the deaths resulted from a misguided attempt by Medea, possibly prompted by Hera, to make them immortal by burying them in Hera's temple.)

In any case, Medea fled to Athens, where she married King Aigeus and, with him, produced a son, Medeios or Medos. Without knowing it, Aigeus had already fathered Theseus on Aithra of Trozen (see note on v. 683 below) and when the boy appeared at Athens to take up the royal succession, Medea tried to get rid of him by having him sent to kill the bull of Marathon. When this scheme failed, in order to protect her own son's rights to the Athenian throne, she tried to poison Theseus, but Aigeus discovered the plot in time and expelled Medea from Athens (a stay by Medea in Athens was noted by the historian Herodotus). She returned to Colchis where her father received her back and forgave her for her earlier crime against the family. A variant version had Aietes' brother Perses ruling in his place. When he tried to imprison Medos, knowing from an oracle that he would be killed by a descendant of his brother, Medea (who in one account had "doubled" Aigeus' failure to recognize Theseus by not realizing that Medos was her son, since the boy had come to Colchis disguised as a son of King Creon of Corinth) gave her son a sword and instructed him to avenge the death of his grandfather Aietes. According to some, Medea eventually joined Achilles in the Elysian Fields.

As an ancient Plot Summary informs us (see p. 80), that part of Medea's story which Euripides dramatized was treated by neither Aeschylus nor Sophocles. But titles survive to indicate that various other episodes described above were handled by them. Aeschylus wrote an *Argo* and his play *Nurses of Dionysus* is mentioned in the Plot Summary (p. 79). To Sophocles are attributed various titles: *Colchidians*, which told of the oath of fidelity given to Medea by Jason—an important element in Euripides' play—and the killing of Apsyrtos; *Scythian Women*, which covered part of the Argonauts' return journey; and *Rhizotomoi* (*Magicians*), which recounted the death of Pelias. Euripides himself dealt with this same episode in his *Daughters of Pelias*, known to have been in the group of plays with which he made his debut as a dramatist in 455 B.C. Medea's sojourn at Athens and attempt on the life of Theseus formed the plot of his *Aigeus*, of unknown date.

The ancient Plot Summary (p. 80) makes the surprising charge that Euripides "seems to have taken over the arrangements [for his *Medea*] from Neophron," citing as authorities for this statement Aristotle and his pupil Dicaearchus. Scholarly controversy has not yet died down over whether there is any truth to the allegation. In vindication of Euripides' priority, it is pointed out that some ancient accounts made Neophron a contemporary of Alexander the Great (who in fact is said to have executed him along with his friend, Callisthenes). On the other hand, it has been felt that so weighty a testimony as Aristotle's cannot simply be ignored. There is no obvious way (known to me, at any rate) of resolving the problem. A few passages are preserved from Neophron's *Medea* which, indeed, show some overlap with Euripides' play. Aigeus appeared, as in vv. 663 ff. below, and for the same reason, to ask Medea to help him solve the Delphic riddle regarding his childlessness. There is a fairly long excerpt corresponding to *Medea* 1019 ff., in which, as in Euripides, Medea wavers between love of her children and a consuming passion for vengeance against Jason; Neophron, too, has Medea address her *thumos* (which I translate "spirit" as if it were an agency acting independently of her, and there is a memorable line: "a madness for murder has infiltrated my great *thumos*." But there is also a marked divergence, for Neophron had Medea predict that Jason would die by his own hand (contrast vv. 1387-8 below), and that this was to be a lesson to "a myriad other mortals not to curse the gods above;" what exactly this was supposed to mean is unclear. One feels—perhaps it is simply showing favorit- ism to Euripides—that if Neophron came first, Euripides improved on him, but that if he followed the converse was not true. If Neophron's version did precede, it means that Medea the murdering mother was not an innovation of Euripides, as some critics maintain.

Besides Neophron's play, whenever it is to be dated, there were tragedies entitled *Medea* that do not survive by various later dramatists, including Carcinus, Dicaeogenes and Euripides the younger (Euripides' nephew) and comedies with that title by, among others, Antiphanes, Eubulus, Strattis and the Sicilian writer of farces, Rhinthon. The story was treated by the Roman dramatists Ennius, Accius and Seneca (whose play survives), as well as by Ovid in his *Metamorphoses* and *Heroides*. Post-classical treatments include Corneille's *Médée* (his first tragedy, 1634-5; he also wrote *La Toison d'Or*, "The Golden Fleece," 1661) and works by Lope de Vega (*El Vellocino de Oro*, published in 1623), Longepierre (1694), the Austrian Grillparzer (*Das goldene Vliess*, published in 1822) and Jean Anouilh (whose *Médée* was composed in 1946 but produced in 1953; Medea kills her children and herself, and her camp- ing-caravan is enveloped in flames). Robinson Jeffers' rendering, which stays quite close to Euripides, achieved much critical acclaim and popular success in America in the late 1940's, when it was a starring vehicle for the great actress Judith Anderson.

Among musical treatments there are works by Cavalli (*Il Giasone*, "Jason," 1649), M.A. Charpentier (1693), Cherubini (1797, following Corneille's text) and Darius Milhaud (1939).

Medea **in the work of Euripides**

There was a popular tradition that Eurpides was born on the day the Greeks won the battle at Salamis, that is, in late September 480 B.C. (Another source places his birth in 484 B.C.) He lived until 406 B.C. and spent his last years in

Macedon, at the invitation of King Archelaos. Eighteen or nineteen of his works survive from a reported total of 92, and yet the record of his successes was no match for that of the other two classic tragedians, for Euripides is reported to have won only five first-place victories (compared with 13 for Aeschylus and perhaps as many as 24 for Sophocles). He began to compete in 455 B.C., as already mentioned, but did not win a first prize until 441. The play translated here dates from ten years later, 431, and as the Plot Summary informs us (p. 81 below), only came in third. Although some modern critics have called it Euripides' masterpiece, and many would rank it among the greatest dramas ever written, in the judgement of its first audience it was a failure. What did they find wrong with it? We can only speculate. At about this same time Euripides produced a play entitled *Hippolytus* (not the one that survives) in which his leading character, Phedra, so shocked the Athenian audience that the author decided to rewrite it, moderating his portrayal of Phedra, and to bring it before them again (the surviving *Hippolytus* of 428 B.C.). It is possible, then, that the audience could not accept the depiction of a mother who murders her former husband's new bride, his father-in-law, and her own children, and so awarded the first prize to one of the other contestants.

There is another possibility. The audience members may simply have been puzzled by the author's intentions. What kind of creature was he presenting to them? In what familiar category of "tragic hero/heroine" were they to place Medea? It is not an easy question for us to answer, and it cannot have been any easier for the original audience. Now, this is not at all to deny that we have before us one of the most powerful creations of the ancient Greek theater, perhaps of the whole range of Western drama. It is just that Medea defies facile classification. Her real nature eludes us. A good deal of the time, particularly in the opening scenes, we think we understand her; she is a woman scorned and rejected, who has sacrificed everything for the man who now, as she repeatedly says, has insulted her, abandoned her, left her helpless in a foreign land. But there is more to it than that, for we hear her talking of her "honor," and using language (as critics have pointed out) appropriate to a male hero operating in the Homeric code of self-worth and the necessity of "saving face" before one's enemies. So an uneasy sense of the contradictions in Medea's character begins to make itself felt. We do not know exactly how to take her. When in the opening scene, for example, the Nurse talks about the relationship that once existed between Medea and Jason, and describes Medea's *thumos*, spirit, as "struck senseless with love of Jason," we may find it hard to believe, but the whole movement of the plot requires us to accept it (otherwise, there would be no justification for Medea's betrayal of her Cholcidian family). Here is a woman whom love could drive to commit terrible crimes for her beloved, and whose love-become-hate will lead her to commit equally horrendous crimes—against, among others, herself. So, too, with her credibilty as a mother. We hear the Nurse in her opening speech say that Medea "hates her children, does not enjoy seeing them" (v. 36), and yet, in the great scene in which she looks in their eyes and fills the stage with the torment she feels at the prospect of killing them (vv. 1019 ff.), surely we must believe that this is a real woman, not a witch with magic powers at her disposal, but a mother who is prepared to violate the deepest instincts of her womanhood, the feelings of protectiveness and nurture towards her children, to get even with the man who violated her trust of him and humiliated her. To quote the Nurse's opening speech once again: she is a "frightening woman; not easily will someone engage with her in hatred and win the prize" (vv. 44-5).

The work presents some other problems and implausibilities. There is the characterization of Jason, so unfeeling and ruthlessly self-interested that it makes nonsense of Medea's claims to "wisdom" that it took her until now to see through him. And the vapid women of the chorus, Corinthians who are prepared to comply with Medea's request to keep mum (v. 263; cf. 267), even after they learn of her intention to launch an assault on the royal family (vv. 374-5). Aigeus' appearance, too, as critics have noted, is too convenient, too unmotivated; and the chariot of the Sun at the end is sheer spectacle. But all these minor blemishes are swept away by the overpowering presence of Medea and the inexorable working out of her evil plan. We are fascinated by her skill, *sophia* (a word used several times of her in the play), and dreadful single-mindedness as she examines every possibility, plans for every contingency, considers and rejects various schemes of revenge, until at last the perfect, most devilish one possible, occurs to her. She must, first, dupe the Corinthian monarch who has ordered her exile into allowing her the breathing space necessary to plan a strategy of attack. Next, she vents her anger and jealousy by killing Jason's bride and her father, too (as it turns out, though that could not be foreseen), using the magic at her disposal to secure for the girl the most painful of deaths, and even exploiting her and Jason's sons as agents. Then there is Jason, with his male vanity and plans to enlarge his family of potential successors. She totally destroys any hopes he might have had of immortality through offspring, even though this means that in killing his children she must also kill her own. Finally, because, after all, her enemies may not have the last laugh, she makes good her escape (with the chlidren's bodies) on her own terms, calling on her family connections with the Sun-god, and thus meeting the conditions set by her Athenian protector.

All this is a terrifying but at the same time breathtakingly beautiful exemplification of the indomitability of the human will, its capacity to fight back from the depths of subjection to others who would trample it and turn it to their own uses. Medea, of all those who have been wronged, strikes back, and in a particularly hideous way. At the play's opening it appears that she is "down for the count" and that the match is over. At the close we are appalled at the totality of the destruction she has wrought. She has turned the tables entirely. So far from her enemies having the laugh on her, she has the laugh—a fiendish and even demonic one, at that—on them. They have learned what it means to "engage with her in hatred." What, however, Medea doesn't see—and this is perhaps her "tragedy"—is that in this combat there have been no winners and that she has lost more than her opponents, for, to mete out the kind of punishment she thinks fitting, she has had to sacrifice everything, even her humanity.

The Design of the Ancient Greek Theater

Drama was not indigenous to Athens, for Herodotus mentions "tragic choruses" (whose exact nature is uncertain) at Sicyon soon after 600 B.C. and other, not so reliable, sources suggest that at about the same time neighboring Corinth enjoyed choral performances, which had perhaps been introduced from Lesbos by the poet Arion; but as in the case of other art-forms, both literary and plastic, the Athenians took what they imported and developed it to a peak of perfection that might have surprised even its originators. Performances of some kind were associated with the name of Thespis and the evidence, while not abundant or uncontroversial, points to the incorporation of "tragedy" into an official civic celebration, involving a contest among competitors and a prize (said to have been a goat; the standard etymology of "tragedy" is "goat-song") about 534 B.C. Probably these early performances took place in the agora, but exactly where has not been determined.

Possibly as early as just after 500 the site of these dramatic competitions was moved to the SE slope of the Acropolis, in a precinct sacred to the god Dionysus, where a permanent theater was later built. At first the spectators sat on the grassy slopes, but soon no doubt temporary wooden stands or "bleachers" were constructed. "Theater" means in origin "viewing place," and what the audience viewed originally has been the subject of much speculation: a circular dancing area of tamped earth, certainly; possibly also a temporary backdrop which, with the addition of some props and unelaborate decoration, could be taken to represent (e.g.) a tomb or council-house, palace or temple. (It is now widely held by scholars that a full scale, permanent scene-building was not constructed until after 460, but Aeschylus' *Persians* of 472 calls for something more or less substantial to serve as the "this ancient structure" referred to by the Chorus at vv. 140-41.) How soon any of this became "graven in stone" is exceedingly unclear. It used to be standard belief that the first stone theater on the site was constructed not very long after 420 B.C., but the archaeologists have in recent years lowered this date considerably, well into the fourth century or even later. Thus Erika Simon writes: "Not until the period of Alexander the Great, under the Attic statesman Lycurgus [that is, about 330 B.C.], was the theater of Dionysus rebuilt in stone" (*The Ancient Theater* as cited below, p 11).

To some extent it is irrelevant what materials were used (R.E. Wycherley allows that the theater of the later fifth century "[was] perhaps already provided with a limited range of stone seating" [p. 210 of his work, *The Stones of Athens*, cited below]. We can be fairly certain that the audience of Euripides' *Medea*, estimated at having been 14,000+ (if it was a full house), sat in wedge-shaped

THEATER OF DIONYSUS

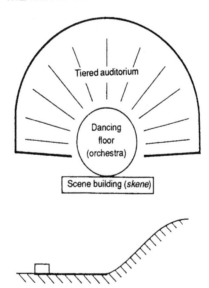

Drawing courtesy of Graham Ley

sections and beheld the action being played out in two essentially separate areas, the dancing circle or "orchestra," which was the special domain of the chorus, and the rectangular stage-area beyond, possibly involving a platform raised several feet above the level of the orchestra and with steps leading down to it, with a single-doored structure representing Medea's house serving as backdrop, where the actors stood and spoke. The building had a flat roof on which, as the situation required, gods might appear at the end (as they frequently do in Euripides' plays); it is possible that Medea's amazing dragon-car was rolled out on this, or the producers (the man who paid to have the chorus outfitted and trained, in collaboration with the dramatist, who did the training) may have availed themselves of a more spectacular mode of conveyance, a crane-like device which was almost certainly in use by the time of Aristophanes' *Peace* of 421 B.C.

From the evidence of vase-paintings it has been deduced that dramatic costumes were quite stylized. Actors wore an elaborately decorated long robe, with a shorter sleeved tunic (white sleeves for female characters) extending to just below the knee. It seems to me likely that Medea would have been costumed in some special way to denote her exotic, "barbarian," origins. One often finds in books the error that the typical tragic footwear, the *kothornos*, was a platform-shoe; it was not, at least in the fifth century (the term seems merely to have designated some kind of special boot or slipper that could fit either foot). Of course, all actors were male, and masked; how exactly these masks were constructed is uncertain, possibly of stiffened linen over a light wooden frame. Again from vase-paintings there seems to have been a progression from fairly straightforward naturalistic masks in the fifth century to a more extreme (and terrifying) style later on involving anguished open mouths and a peaked hairdo.

The evidence in clearly presented and discussed judiciously by R.E. Wycherley, *The Stones of Athens* (Princeton, 1978) 263 ff. Further references: A.W. Pickard-Cambridge, *The Theater of Dionysus at Athens* (Oxford, 1946) and *The Dramatic Festivals of Athens*, 2nd edition revised by J. Gould and D. M. Lewis (Oxford, 1968); Erika Simon, *The Ancient Theater*, English translation by C.E. Vafopoulou-Richardson (London and New York, 1982); Leo Aylen, *The Greek Theater* (Rutherford, N. J. and London, 1985); Peter D. Arnott, *Public and Performance in the Greek Theater* (London and New York, 1989); Bernhard Zimmermann, *Greek Tragedy, an Introduction*, English translation by Thomas Marier (Baltimore and London, 1991); Rush Rehm, *Greek Tragic Theatre* (London and New York, 1992); Graham Ley, *A Short Introduction to the Ancient Greek Theater* (Chicago, 1991) (my thanks also to Graham Ley for the diagram on p. 10).

Euripides' *Medea*°

Characters

Nurse
Creon, King of Corinth
Children of Medea
Tutor
Jason
Chorus of Corinthian Women
Aigeus, King of Athens
Medea
Messenger

(The scene° is a street in Corinth. Medea's house is in the background. An elderly female, Medea's "Nurse"—that is, personal maid—steps out of the front door and addresses the audience.)

NURSE°

I wish that the ship Argo° had never flown
Through the dark, Clashing rocks° to the land of Colchis,°

The translation was made originally from D.L. Page's edition (Oxford, 1938; reprinted), but has been revised in light of J. Diggle's Oxford text (1984) (cf. also David Kovacs, ed. and trans., *Euripides: Cyclops, Alcestis, Medea* (Loeb Library, Cambridge and London, 1994).

The *scene* is before a house in Corinth, evidently that in which Jason and Medea had lived with their two boys (not named in the play; later accounts name them as Pheres and Mermeros) before Jason's withdrawal to the palace.

Nurse. As often in Euripides, a character appears and gives some background information. Here it is Medea's "Nurse," that is, personal maid, who explains that Medea's present troubles can be traced back to the time when Jason set out from Thessaly with the Argonautic expedition to the land of Colchis, where he met Medea and with her help secured the Golden Fleece (see Introduction).

1. *The ship Argo:* the vessel built by the "Argonauts" under Athena's inspiration for the quest of the Golden Fleece.

2. *Clashing rocks:* they are sometimes identified with the *Planktai*, or "Wandering Rocks," which Homer mentions. These reefs, at the western end of the Black Sea near the mouth of the Bosporus, were believed to shift their position inexplicably, and so were particularly treacherous to sailors. (The phenomenon described appears to have been discovered in some offshore rocky islands quite often covered in a low mist; see W.F. Pickard in *Greece and Rome* 34 [1987] 1-6).

Colchis: on the eastern shore of the Black Sea.

That in the forest glens of Mt. Pelion° the pine
Had never been cut for her, had never been made
Into oars for the hands of excellent sailors who hunted   5
The Golden Fleece for Pelias.° My lady,
Medea, would never have sailed to Iolkos'° towers,
Her spirit struck senseless° with love of Jason.
She wouldn't have persuaded Pelias' daughters° to kill
Their father; she wouldn't have settled here in Corinth,   10
With her husband and children. She tried to please
The people to whose land she had come, an exile,
And for her part to fit in with Jason in everything.
This, to my mind, is a woman's greatest safety:
Not to take the opposite side from her husband.   15
But now—everything's hateful, her love is sick.
Jason betrayed his children and my mistress
For the marriage-bed of a royal bride; he's married
The daughter of Creon, the ruler of the country.
And Medea – poor woman! – treated with dishonor,°   20
Shouts "Where are the oaths? Your right hand given
In trust?" She calls upon the gods to witness
What kind of return she has received from Jason.

---

3. *Mt. Pelion:* a mountain in southeast Thessaly, from which the Argonauts set sail. In their war against the Olympian gods the giants attempted to pile the neighboring Mt. Ossa on Pelion to scale the heights of Olympus.

6. *Golden Fleece for Pelias:* Jason's uncle Pelias had treacherously deprived his half-brother, and Jason's father, of the kingdom of Iolkos (v. 7). When Jason turned up to claim the throne, Pelias attempted to get him out of the way by insisting that he perform an apparently impossible "labor," fetching the fabulous fleece of a golden ram from faraway Colchis (he later reneged on his promise to turn the kingdom over to Jason if the latter were successful in his quest).

7. *Iolkos:* modern Volo, on Thessaly's southern coast, seat of Pelias' kingdom.

8. *her spirit struck senseless:* it seems difficult to believe that the Medea we see in this play, coolly calculating the best means of revenging herself on those who have wronged her, could ever have been "swept away" by her love for Jason. But that is what the story requires and is certainly one of the features of the myth as it is told by other writers.

9. *Pelias' daughters:* when Pelias refused to give up his rule to his nephew, who had successfully carried out the assigned task (see note on v. 6), Medea devised a terrible scheme to remove him. Having first demonstrated her magic abilities by rejuvenating a ram, she persuaded Pelias' daughters to cut up their father and boil him, promising them that this would have the effect of renewing his youth. It did not. (She refers to her misdeed several times in the play; see vv. 485-6 and 504-5).

20. *Treated with dishonor:* this in particular is what rankles in Medea's soul; besides the thought of all she has given up for what now turns out to have been a bad bargain (v. 23), and her very human feeling of helplessness and inferiority at having her male support removed—not to mention sheer jealousy—her honor also is a stake (see also v. 33).

She doesn't eat,° surrenders to her sorrows;
Her life has been turned into a river of tears   25
Since realizing the wrong her husband does her;
She keeps her gaze fixed on the ground, never
Looking up. She listens to friends' advice
No more than a rock or wave of the sea.
Oh, sometimes she'll turn her white cheek away   30
To herself, and let out a wail for her dear father,
Her country, her home,° which she betrayed to come
With her husband, who has now so dishonored° her.
She understands, poor woman, from what has happened
How important it is not to leave one's homeland.   35
She hates her children,° does not enjoy seeing them.
I'm afraid she may be planning something rash.
Her mind is dangerous. She will not endure
Mistreatment. I know this woman and fear her;   39
She's a frightening woman: not easily will someone   44
Engage with her in hatred and win the prize.°   45

(Medea's two young sons rush in, accompanied by their "tutor," or attendant slave.)°

But here come the boys who have just finished
Their running. They're not thinking about their mother's
Troubles. For young minds aren't used to suffering.

---

24. *she doesn't eat:* similarly Phedra in *Hippolytus* (135 ff.); it is a dangerous sign when Euripidean women behave this way.

31-2. *dear father…home:* the terrible crime of violating a close blood-bond is compounded by the thought that, at the pragmatic level, there is "no way back" for her. (She often returns to the topic; see, e.g. vv. 166, 596 ff. etc).

33. *so dishonored:* see note on v. 20

36. *she hates her children:* a first hint (but as yet no more than that) that her grief and rage may be turned against her children.

38-43. This entire passage is condemned by Diggle, and others. I agree that 40-43 are probably spurious, since they are vague, weak and repetitious, but I believe that 38 and 39 should be retained.

45. *win the prize:* with the alteration accepted by Diggle the text will mean "sing a victory-song."

(Medea's two young sons...), accompanied by a "tutor," in fact, a slave whose function was to accompany male children in the normal round of their day's activities, lessons, exercises, etc. The scene which follows presents a lively and realistic dialogue between the two household slaves; the information that the Tutor brings regarding the King's edict of banishment could have been presented in fewer lines but the overall effect is of a relatively tranquil domestic scene (with only a few forebodings) before the storm breaks with Medea's entrance.

Tutor

You, my mistress' long-time household slave,
Why are you standing here all by yourself   50
Outside, crying out loudly about your troubles?
How is it that Medea is willing to be without you?

Nurse

Old man, attendant and tutor of Jason's children,
When masters' affairs take an unlucky turn,
Good slaves feel it, too, and have sorrowful hearts.   55
I have come to such a pitch of suffering
That a longing filled me to come outside and tell
The earth and sky about my mistress' sorrows.

Tutor

Has she not yet, poor woman, stopped her wailing?

Nurse

I envy you! Trouble's starting, not at the half!   60

Tutor

Foolish—if one may use this word of masters;
How unaware she is of the latest evils!

Nurse

What is it, old man? Don't grudge me your news.

Tutor

Nothing. I've changed my mind about what I said.

Nurse

I beg you not to hide it from your fellow-slave.   65
If necessary, I can be quiet about it.

Tutor

Without appearing to listen, I heard it said,
As I came to the place called "Dice" where the very old
Sit and play, near the sacred spring of Peirene,°
That the king of this country, Creon, was going to issue   70
An edict exiling these children from the land of Corinth
Along with their mother. Whether this report was correct,
I don't know. But I wish it were not so.

---

69. *Peirene:* Corinth's sacred spring which began on the height of Acrocorinth and ran down to the lower city.

Nurse

> Jason surely will not tolerate such treatment
> Of his children, even though at odds with their mother?   75

Tutor

> Old marriage-bonds are left behind by new ones,
>
> *(He points to Medea's house.)*
>
> And he has no friendly feelings for this house.

Nurse

> We're ruined, then, if we must add a new
> Evil to the old one we've hardly saved ourselves from.

Tutor *(somewhat threateningly)*

> But you must keep still and be quiet about the report,   80
> Since this isn't the time for the mistress to learn it.

Nurse *(drawing the boys to her)*

> Children, do you hear what a father you've got? Damn
> —I won't say him; for he is still my master,
> But he's been caught being evil to his dear ones.

Tutor

> And what human being *hasn't* been? Did you just find out   85
> That each man loves himself more than his neighbor?°   86
> If their father doesn't love them because of this marriage…   88
>
> *(Nurse attempts to shield the children)*

Nurse

> Go into the house, children, all will be well.
> And you *(to Tutor)* keep them apart as far as possible;   90
> Don't bring them near their angry mother.
> For I just now saw her casting savage° looks
> At them, as if to do something. She won't cut short

85-86. A surprising bit of cynicism for the Tutor. To some extent it exonerates Jason: he is just doing what most (all?) men do, put themselves first. It reminds us how exceptional Medea is: she gave herself over to her passion wholly and to some extent against her interest (and her reversed feelings will be just as all-consuming and self-destructive).

87. This line is omitted in the translation ("some men with justice, and others for the sake of profit"). An ancient marginal note condemns it and it is both banal and inappropriate here.

92. *savage:* more literally, "like a bull." We are given another, more ominous indication of the ugly turn events will later take.

Her wrath, I'm sure, until it strikes against someone.°
May she do something to enemies, though, not friends.   95

(From 96 to 213 the Nurse and Chorus outside and Medea within engage in an antiphonal exchange, half-sung, half-chanted. Medea's savage grief reverberates against the old servant's mounting terror.)

Medea *(inside)*

Oh!
I'm miserable and wretched with suffering,
Oh! Oh! I wish I could die.

Nurse

There, I told you, dear children,
Your mother stirs her heart, stirs her wrath.
Hasten quickly into the house   100
And don't come into her sight;°
Don't come near her, but watch out
For the savage bent°, the hateful nature
Of her self-willed° mind.
Go now, go quickly inside.   105

(They start towards the door, puzzled, but do not enter.)

Clearly her groans are just the beginning:°
The cloud of her grief starts, is rising,
Will kindle to flames when her spirit fans it
To greater fury. What will it do,
That deeply brooding, inexorable soul,
Stung by wrongs it has suffered?   110

(The children have now entered the house with the Tutor.)

---

94. *strikes against someone:* like a thunderbolt, as Flacelière suggests.

101. *don't come into her sight:* her look had been described as "bull-like" (note on v. 92) and there is a suggestion that the boys, by allowing themselves to be seen by their mother, will somehow activate or trigger some savage burst of destructive energy, as if her generalized anger will focus on them if she sees them. (Medea will later be very much affected, almost disarmed, by her children's gaze, vv. 1040-3.)

103. *savage bent:* we are being prepared for a Medea whose actions will be less than human ("no more than a rock or wave of the sea," v. 29)

104. *self-willed:* this is a key word in understanding Medea's motivation. She will not follow in the normal path that most women take; she showed imaginative individuality in a destructive way before (at Colchis and Iolkos), and it would be surprising if her atypicality did not manifest itself again in some farfetched, hardly imaginable way.

106-7. *Just the beginning…is rising:* cf. v. 60.

Medea

> Ah…!
> I suffered—miserable—suffered things
> Deserving loud laments. Accursed
> Children° of a hateful mother!
> Perish with your father!
> The whole house be damned!

Nurse

> Ah! I am the one who is miserable.   115
> What share do your children have° in their father's
> Sin? Why do you hate them? Oh,
> Children, how I grieve for what you may suffer.
> Terrible is the temperament of royalty,
> Who are rarely controlled, always imperious;   120
> It is hard for them to give up their wrath.
> To get used to living like everybody else
> Is better; I at any rate hope
> To grow old securely° in simple surroundings.
> "Moderate" first wins a prize   125
> For the sound it has; then it's far the best
> For humans to live by. Excess on the other hand
> Always surpasses what is appropriate for men.
> When heaven gets angry at a house
> It pays back ruin in plenty.   .   130

(The chorus members, fifteen in number, who represent the women of Corinth, enter along one or both entrance ways [if one, probably the western, stage-left, one] and eventually take up their position in the orchestra, or dancing-place.)

113-4. *Accursed Children:* Surprisingly strong language; as products of a passionate love-gone-sour they stir their mother to equally passionate anger, but we suspect also that Euripides is preparing the audience for the outcome (see vv. 36 and 92, with notes).

116. *What share do your children have…?:* Of course, this is "Everyperson's" viewpoint. Medea's reasoning is peculiar, stranger, for she is not (although she sometimes talks like) "Everywoman."

119 ff. *the temperament of royalty…I at any rate hope To grow old securely:* it is not clear what prompts this disquisition by the Nurse (unless it is that Medea, as "royalty" displaced, has the sort of imperious temperament that the Nurse here warns against). This kind of homespun sententiousness is very common, not only in Euripides but in the other dramatists. Here it serves to emphasize the gap between the great mythic figures who walk the stage and the ordinary members of the audience (the phenomenon of tragic "catharsis," as it is called, requires that the gap be a large one—the hero's or heroine's suffering is on a gigantic and almost abnormal scale—but not entirely unbridgeable, for the audience must feel "what it must be like" to be an Oedipus or a Medea).

Choral Entrance Song°

I heard the voice, I heard the shout
Of the unfortunate Colchian woman.° Is she not yet
Calm?° Tell me old woman.
For I was inside on the porch when I heard   135
The wailing°, and I find no joy
In the household's sufferings,
For it has a fixed place in my heart.

Nurse

The household has crumbled. It is no more.
He is held fast in the royal bed   140
While she, my mistress, secluded in her chamber,
Pines her life away; her heart will not be warmed
By any word from friends.

Medea *(still within)*

Ah!…
I wish my head° could be struck by a bolt
From above! What good for me to live longer?   145
Oh, Oh. I wish my hateful life
Would dissolve in death.

Chorus

Do you hear, Zeus and earth and light?
Do you hear the song the bride is
Wailing° so miserably?   150
Foolish woman, why long for the terrible
Resting place?
Why hasten the end of death?
Do not pray for this.

---

131. *Choral Entrance Song.* The chorus, fifteen "ordinary" Corinthian women, enter singing in lyric meters; Medea (who is still secluded in the house) and the Nurse interject remarks in anapaests, which might have been chanted rather than spoken. The whole effect is one of stylized and contrapuntal formality.

133. *unfortunate …woman (and 143, word from friends):* the Chorus are on Medea's side, which helps to explain why they so readily agree to her request for silence later.

132-3. I accept Diggle's punctuation of these lines as a question.

136. "Wailing" is Elmsley's emendation for the manuscripts' "shouting."

144. *I wish my head…:* the vehemence of Medea's language is noteworthy (the chorus thus have their answer to their question at vv. 132-3).

149-50. *song the bride is Wailing:* a favorite type of paradox in Greek poetry (and of course Medea is no longer a "bride").

If your husband now shows reverence for   155
A new bridal bed,
Do not rage at him for it.
Zeus will see that you get your due.
Save your tears. Do not lament for
Your former partner too much.

Medea

O great goddess, Justice,° and lady Artemis,   160
Do you see what I suffer,
Even though I bound my accursed husband
With mighty oaths? I wish I could see him
And his bride crushed, house and all,
For the wrong that—unprovoked—they dare to inflict on me.   165
Father! City!° How shameful it was
To kill my brother° and leave you!

Nurse

Do you hear how she cries out
Her prayer to Justice and Zeus,° whom
Men consider the steward of oaths?   170
There is no possible way my mistress'
Rancor will just trickle away.

Chorus

If only she would come out
Where I could see her,
Talk to her,   175
Try to relieve the heavy weight of wrath
On her heart.
My eager concern
Must never fail my friends.
(To nurse) Go, bring her here out of the house.   180
Tell her we are her friends.

---

160. *great goddess, Justice:* the word in Greek is *Themis*, a very old personification embodying a natural and quasi-religious (as opposed to legal and somewhat arbitrary) justice. Artemis was typically a woman's patron divinity, who supervised childbirth and other female activities.

166. *Father! City!...:* recollection of the terrible wrong done to her family once again sears her soul (see vv. 32-3, with note)

167. *to kill my brother:* Apsyrtos, whose severed limbs Medea had scattered from the Argo to delay her father's pursuit (see Introduction and, below, v. 1334).

169. *her prayer to Justice and Zeus:* The chorus had called upon Zeus (vv. 148, 158), but Medea, so far, has not. A minor inconsistency, but the reason for it is unclear.

Quick! before she does some harm°
To those inside. For her sorrow is surging greatly.

Nurse

All right—but I fear I may not persuade
My mistress.   185
A nuisance, but I shall do you this favor.
Yet she glares at her servants
Like a mother lioness,° when anyone
Comes near her to speak.
You'd be right if you called those men   190
Of the past stupid and gauche
Who contrived the sweet
Sounds of song° for parties,
Banquets and feasts.
But nobody found how to stop human suffering   195
With music and pleasant songs,
To save their families from destruction and death.
Yet to cure *these* by singing
Would be profit indeed.
Why sing loud and long   200
When a feast succeeds on its own?
The party itself brings men joy
In full measure.

Chorus

I heard the shriek,   205
The sorrowful wailing;
She cries out shrilly, painfully,
That her husband wrongs and betrays her.
She calls on Zeus' daughter, Justice, protectress of oaths,
Who brought her° over to Greece,   210
Over the dark sea to the briny
Bosporus, gateway of the vast Euxine.

---

182. *before she does some harm:* a further suggestion that the children are in danger.

188. *like a mother lioness:* once again an indication that there is something inhuman, even bestial, about Medea's frame of mind; see vv. 29, 92, 103.

192 ff. *the sweet sounds of song:* an interesting bit of introspection by a poet, an assessment of the limitations of his art. The thought, however, which continues for some lines, seems to be somewhat labored here.

209-10. *Justice, protectress of oaths, who brought her:* Medea denounced Jason as a "breaker of oaths" (vv. 21-2, 162-3); here, she bitterly reproaches those divinities whose job it is to guarantee such oaths, and who in her case appear not to have done so. She will take matters into her own hands.

(Enter Medea)°

Women of Corinth, I have come out of the house
To avoid your reproaches. I know that many men   215
Are really haughty, some where none can see them,
Others openly. Some get a bad reputation
Simply from living a life of ease and comfort.
People do not behave justly in hating
Another on sight, with no injury done,   220
Without learning fully the person's character.°
An alien, too,° must especially blend with the city;
But I don't approve, either, of the citizen who,
Self-willed and boorish, gives offence to others.
This thing has fallen on me like a bolt from nowhere,°   225
Destroying my soul. I'm ruined. The joy of living
Is gone for me. I want to die, my friends.
The one who was everything to me (I know it)
Has turned out the worst of men, my husband.
    Of all creatures that live and have understanding°   230

---

214. (*Enter Medea*) This speech is very different from what we might have expected, given the lengthy descriptions of Medea's pent-up fury and her own raptures of grief. Obviously, one intended effect is surprise. Something else has troubled readers and critics: Why does she sound so ordinary, uttering what are almost platitudes (though true), and sounding more like Everywoman—and Greek Everywoman, at that—than a Black Sea witch? Many have thought her reasonable tone and careful, even tedious, argumentation nothing more than a façade; she is not at all like this, as we and the characters in the drama will soon discover. In my opinion, it is likelier that we are being asked to believe in her as a woman scorned and, as a foreign woman would be in most Greek cities of the time, totally vulnerable. If we feel sympathy for her, I believe we are meant to. She has been dealt with callously, treacherously, even, and has (literally) nowhere to turn. She must, then, reach deep into a wholly different and utterly dark side of her nature to devise an escape from this situation.

215-21. The inconsequentiality of this section in particular (see preceding note) has struck many critics. An explanation can be found (at least in part) in the fact that by this time the Athenians were evolving elaborate schemes for constructing a persuasive speech, and that an extended proem or "warm-up" was a required feature of this highly formalized style of speechwriting—witness some of the speeches in Thucydides. Otherwise, we can say that she is really just trying to make the Corinthian women think that she is completely normal and even a bit chatty, to take them off the scent of her real intentions.

222. *an alien, too:* now we come to a point that is relevant to her own situation (although in 223-4 she veers again to inconsequentiality).

225. *like a bolt from nowhere:* the Greek is not quite so specific, but it seems legitimate to interpret it in light of v. 94.

230 ff. It is hard to imagine a stronger or more crystalline statement of the position put forward in the following twenty lines; they have rightly been considered a "classic" presentation of women's social vulnerability, and their applicability has extended beyond the Greece of Euripides' day.

We women are the wretchedest breed alive;
First, we must use excessive amounts of cash°
To buy our husbands, and what we get are masters
Of our bodies. This is the worst pain of all.
In fact, this is no small struggle,° whether he'll be   235
A good or bad one, for divorce brings no repute
To wives, and yet they can't deny their husbands.°
So coming into new rules and customs,
She must be a prophet, since she hasn't learnt at home°
How to deal in the best way with her bed-mate.   240
And if we manage to find a solution to this,
So husbands live with and don't feel chained to us,
Our lives are a joy; if not, it is better to die.
But a man, when life with his family oppresses him,
Can turn to others° to relieve his heart's distress,   245
Either to a friend or men of his own age.°
We must look to only one other person.
They say that we spend all our time at home,
And live safe lives, while they go out to battle.
What fools they are! I'd rather stand three times°   250
Behind a shield, than bear a child once!

---

232. *excessive amounts of cash:* the reference is to the dowry, which was often a considerable amount.

235. *no small struggle:* for of course, in an arranged marriage, the wife had little say in the choice of husband.

236-7. For a Greek man, divorce was a relatively simple matter: he simply went before a magistrate and made known his intention. For a Greek woman it was much more difficult to initiate, and involved a complicated legal process.

239. *she hasn't learnt at home:* another complaint of more general applicability. A girl marrying generally in her mid or late teens must have been ignorant in some essential matters. (It could, however, also be argued that the male, too, was sexually immature. Though considerably older than his wife, his experience would have been limited by the fact that most of his social life was among members of his own sex.)

244-5. *a man…can turn to others:* even more true in Euripides' day than perhaps at later periods. The opportunities for a Greek woman in the fifth century to initiate any kind of social contact on her own were virtually non-existent.

246. Diggle follows Wilamowitz in condemning this verse; unnecessarily, it seems to me ("a friend" and "men of his own age" are not co-extensive, so there is no redundancy, and the verse fills out the preceding one, 245, which is rather abrupt without it).

250-1. *I'd rather stand three times…:* it is difficult to imagine a more lapidary statement of the sentiment expressed in these famous epigrammatic lines.

But your reasoning is no doubt different from mine:
This is your city; you have fathers' homes;
You enjoy life and the company of friends.
I am alone and stateless°; my husband insults me.° 255
I was brought from a foreign land, a piece of plunder;
I have no mother or brother or kinsman° to go to
For shelter from my present adversity.
I only ask to obtain° so much from you:
If some method or scheme can be found for me 260
To pay my husband back for these sufferings,
His father-in-law and the girl he married,°
Keep silent. A woman is generally full of fear,
And cowardly, when facing armed aggression;
But when she's been wronged in anything touching sex, 265
No mind is more homicidal than hers.°

Chorus

I'll do as you ask. Justly, Medea, you'll pay
Your husband back. No wonder you grieve for what's happened.
But I see Creon, ruler of this country,
Coming here to announce some new decision.° 270

(Enter Creon, with attendants.)°

253-5. *This is your city…I am alone and stateless:* Medea turns to a new point. As a foreigner, even if she were Greek, she would have no civic status without a male citizen to represent her interests.

my husband insults me: a very strong formulation which in other contexts might even imply "rapes me."

257. *no mother or brother or kinsman:* in the case of legal divorce, this much protection was afforded the female: she could return to her nearest male kinsman for protection (taking her dowry with her). Medea has of course forfeited this (see v. 167).

259. *I only ask to obtain…:* in the view of some critics, Medea's long arguments thus far have been only posturing; she has been systematically ingratiating herself, pulling at the women's heart-strings, to elicit this promise that they do nothing to interfere with her revenge-plot, not even reveal it. There may be some truth to this view, but I think that it is easy to overstate the extent of her insincerity so far (see note on v. 214, *Enter Medea*)

262. This line is condemned by many editors.

263-6. A splendid, vigorous cap to this fine speech (although 264 seems to contradict 251). She closes her address with a blood-curdling epigram.

270. *some new decision:* they may have heard the same rumor as the Tutor (vv. 67 ff.), or this is simply an anticipation.

Enter Creon….) There is some evidence that there was a conventional distinction between the two entrance-ways to mark the direction from which the entering person was coming (or to which he or she was going). If so, Creon will enter from the western (stage-left) entrance, which marked arrivals from and departures to the city or harbor (east denoted the countryside).

Creon

You! The scowling hater of your husband,
Medea, I order you to go from this land
An exile, and take your two children with you.
And no delay! For I'm the one who gives
The orders here, and I won't go home again°   275
Until I've cast you outside the country's borders.

Medea

Oh! How wretched and utterly ruined° I am!
For my enemies are letting out all their sail,
And no ready harbor° from ruin awaits me.
Though you've treated me foully, I shall still ask: 280
For what reason are you driving me out, Creon?

Creon

I fear you°—no need to dress up the language—
Fear you'll work some incurable harm to my daughter;
And many things contribute to this fear:
You're clever and much versed in doing harm,   285
And you're suffering the lack of your husband's bed.
I hear you've threatened°—that's the report that came—
To do something ...*that's* what I must guard against.
It's better for me to feel your anger now,   290
Than lament loudly later for showing softness.

---

274 ff. *I'm the one who gives The orders here...I won't go home again:* I think that the poet gives
such heavy emphasis not to portray Creon as a spluttering state-autocrat, but to show how
massively opposed to Medea are the political forces of Corinth. It will take all her ingenuity
(or another demonstration of her fabled magic) to overcome such opposition. The fact that
Creon does "go home again" without having expelled her, but against his better judgement,
shows how skillful Medea is at manipulating her male adversaries. Jason will later step into
a similar trap.

277. *How wretched and utterly ruined:* a conventional but effective feminine appeal.

278-9. *have let out their sails...no ready harbor:* imagery from seafaring is pervasive in Greek
poetry (cf. vv. 523-4, 769-70).

282. *I fear you:* Creon's instincts are correct. He senses Medea's capacity for working "incurable
harm." That she succeeds in spite of this shows how skilled she is at getting her own way
(even in human terms). It also adds another undertone of foreboding, a covert warning that
springs of malign power lie just beneath her smooth surface.

287. *I hear you've threatened:* when (in stage time) should we conceive of Medea as having made
these threats? Probably before the action begins. See also vv. 457-8. (I have excised v. 288
on grounds of, among other things, its similarity to v. 262.)

Medea

Oh! Oh!
This isn't the first time° Creon, it's happened often,
That reputation has injured and done me much harm.
A man who's naturally sensible should never
Bring up his children to be excessively wise.   295
Apart from the charge of idleness they get,
They earn hatred and jealousy from the citizens.
If you bring some new wisdom to stupid men
You'll seem to them useless and not wise;
From being considered better than those who have   300
Some subtle skill, you'll appear offensive to all.
This is the very thing that's happened to me;
Since I'm a wise woman,° some are jealous,   303
Others annoyed, yet I'm not over-wise.   305
You fear me—fear something unpleasant?
Don't be afraid of me, Creon, I haven't the means
To do harm to men who are the rulers.
What wrong did you do to me? You gave your daughter
To whom your spirit urged you. My husband's the one   310
I hate. You acted sensibly, I think,
And now I don't begrudge your affairs prospering;
Go on with the marriage! Be happy! But allow me to live
In this country. For although we've been treated unjustly,
We'll say nothing; we've lost out to our betters.   315

Creon

Soothing words you've spoken, but in my mind
There lurks a fear° that you're planning something bad.

292-301. *This isn't the first time…etc.:* again, Medea begins in a very roundabout and "rhetorical" way. Perhaps (although this is far from certain; see note on 214, *Enter Medea*) this is meant to characterize her as being able to feign pompous longwindedness to put her opponent off the scent. (My hesitations to describe it in this way stem from the fact that such rhetoricizing is common in Euripides, even when there seems to be no effort to characterize his speaker, as, for example, Hippolytus.)

303. *Since I'm a wise woman:* picks up Creon's charge at v. 285. By harping on this topic of "wisdom" or "cleverness" (the Greek word is the same), Medea hopes to deflect fears that her skills, for which she was evidently renowned, may be put to harmful use against the royal family.

304. This verse (almost duplicated at v. 808) has been omitted from the translation, since it interrupts the line of argument.

316-7. *in my mind There lurks a fear:* once again (cf v. 282) Creon's instincts are to be wary. His generalization at vv. 319-20 is correct: now that Medea has got control of herself, she is much more potentially dangerous than when she was "carried away" by her grief and anger.

I trust you, then, by that much less than before.
A woman, just like a man, who is quick to wrath
Is easier guarded than one wise and silent.   320
Leave, go away at once; no further talk.
Since this is settled, you cannot devise a way°
To remain here, since you wish me harm.

Medea

Don't, I implore you by your daughter's marriage!

Creon

You're wasting words; you'll never be able to sway me.   325

Medea

You'll drive me out? You'll not respect my prayers?

Creon

I cannot love you more than my own family.

Medea

O country of mine,° how I remember you now!

Creon

By far the dearest thing to me, after children.°

Medea

Ah! What an evil thing men's loves° are!   330

Creon

It all depends, I suppose, on how things turn out.

Medea

Zeus,° I hope you notice the source of these wrongs.

Creon

Go, you foolish woman; end my suffering!

---

322. *you cannot devise a way:* how wrong he is!

328. *O country of mine:* now that it appears that she must leave Corinth, and today, the thought
that she literally has no place to go has its maximum impact on her (see vv. 32-3, with note;
166-7).

329. *after children:* an allusion to the importance of children, not only to Creon here, but later:
to Aigeus, to Jason, to Medea herself.

330. *men's loves:* especially, as we are given ironically to understand, when, as in her case, they
have gone wrong.

332. *Zeus:* now at last she does call upon the Father of gods (see note on v. 169).

Medea

And what of mine? Who will relieve me of it?°

Creon *(motions to attendants)*

An attendant here will take you away by force.   335

Medea *(grasping him in supplication)*

Do not, I beg you, Creon, resort to this.

Creon

You're making trouble for nothing, it seems, woman.

Medea

I'll go into exile. I'm not pleading for pardon.

Creon

Well, why not simply leave without resisting?

Medea

A single day° allow me to remain   340
To think through where I shall go in exile
And find some means of life for my children. Their father
Sets no stock on devising something° for them.
Have pity on them! You are a father, too.°
It's natural for you to show them° kindness.   345
My concern isn't for me if we go into exile;
My tears are rather for them and their misfortunes.

Creon

My nature is not tyrannical in the least;°
I've already lost much through being sensitive;
I see the mistake I'm making now, woman,   350
Yet you shall have this—but I'm warning you,
If the rays of the coming dawn shall look upon you

---

334. I agree with Diggle that the text is faulty as it stands. I offer a translation of what (prob-ably) the author intended.

340. *A single day:* Medea's trump card; who could resist such an apparently trifling request?

343. *sets no stock on devising something:* but Jason will show some fatherly feelings (vv. 460-1).

344. *You are a father, too:* Medea picks up Creon's point at v. 329; we will be reminded again, in a gruesome way, of his affectionate nature at vv. 1204 ff.

345. *to show them:* I translate Vitelli's conjecture, which Diggle adopts.

348 ff. Euripides goes to an extreme in presenting his secondary character in a favorable, even sympathetic, light. When Creon says, "I see the mistake I'm making," he uses a conventional phrase that is sometimes uttered by other, genuinely tragic, figures.

And the children within the boundaries of this land,
You'll die; this sentence is passed unerringly.
So remain, if you must, but only for one day.   355
You'll not do any of the terrible things I fear.°

(Exit Creon)

Chorus

Poor woman,°
Oh, where ever will you go
Overcome by your sufferings?
To what hospitable house   360
Or land to save you from harm?
How God has placed you in the way
Of a wave of harm, with no way out!°

Medea

Everything's totally ruined—there's no denying—°
O, but don't suppose only for me.   365
Struggles still await the newlyweds
And sufferings for their kinsmen, not small ones.
Do you suppose I'd ever have flattered that man
Unless devising something for my profit?
I'd never have talked to or touched him with my hands.   370
But he arrived at such a pitch of folly
That, even though he might have spoiled my plans
By exiling me, he allowed me to remain
This day, in which I'll make three people
Corpses:° father, daughter, and my husband.   375

355-6. Critics since Nauck have condemned this couplet as a weak repetition of what Creon has already said. But people repeat themselves in real life. Besides, the poignancy of the "just one day" theme—so near and yet so far—may bear repetition. And it would be a pity to lose the irony of v. 356, which seems to me indisputably Euripidean.

357-63. The Chorus (or perhaps just the Leader) chant an anapaestic stanza here (I translate the traditional order of verses, not Diggle's transposition).

363. *with no way out:* but Medea, with demonic and self-destructive inventiveness, will discover one.

364 ff. In this great speech Medea flings off the mask of fawning servility and feminine help-lessness which she had put on to dupe Creon. We begin to hear the colossal pride which has sustained so severe a wound, and the rage which wells up from deep within her. Her enemies will soon discover the strength of her willpower and of her determination not to let such affronts go unavenged.

374-5. *I'll make three people Corpses:* later the plan will be changed; she does not kill Jason (in any literal sense, that is), and cannot have foreseen Creon's death; this fits in with the rumored threats about which we have already heard (vv. 287-9).

I have so many ways of killing them,°
I don't know which I'll try out first, my friends.
Perhaps I'll set fire to the bridal chambers,
Or drive a sharpened dagger through their sides,
Entering in silence the room where the bed is spread.   380
But one pitfall, there, for me: if I'm caught
Creeping into the house° and plotting something,
My death will give my enemies a laugh.°
Best to take the direct route, where my natural
Skills can shine: murder them with poisons.   385
Well, then;
Let's say they've died. What city will accept me?
What foreign host will offer me asylum
In guaranteed safety, and defend my person?
There is none. I'll wait a little while longer,
And if some tower of refuge° appears for me   390
I'll proceed to the crime with silence and deceit.
But if an unmanageable disaster drives me away,
I'll take the knife myself, even to die,
And murder them, and move with force and daring.
No, by the mistress whom I most revere   395
Of all, and chose to help me in my work,
Hecate°, who lives in the recesses of my hearth,
They'll not make my heart hurt and get off free!
Bitter and painful I shall make their marriage,
Bitter the marriage-connection and my exile.   400
Well, Medea,° spare none of the things

---

376. *I have so many ways of killing them:* so this is not murder without premeditation.

381-2. *if I'm caught Creeping into the house:* again, a very rational calculation (and in any case, such crude means seem unsuitable for a "wise" or "clever" murderess).

383. *My death will give my enemies a laugh:* this is the typical "heroic" stance, not to become a laughing-stock to one's enemies, and so humiliated as well as vulnerable; see vv. 404, 797, 1049.

390. *some tower of refuge:* as we shall see, this is just what will happen with the arrival of King Aigeus at v. 663.

395-7. *The mistress…Hecate:* in some versions of the story, Medea was a priestess of this underworld goddess, who taught her the art of witchcraft. According to one late account Hecate had married Aietes and was the mother of Medea and Circe.

401. *Well, Medea:* for a hero or heroine to address himself or herself by name is rather unusual. Perhaps it is intended to remind the audience that hers is a significant name, "She-who-devises."

You know, none of your schemings and devices.
Advance to the terrible! Now it's a test of courage.°
You see what they're doing to you? You mustn't be laughed at°
By these Sisyphian marriages° of Jason,   405
Since your father was noble, and his father, the Sun.°
You know how.

(turns to Chorus, conspiratorially)
                    And what is more,
We're women, quite unable to manage good,
But none more skilled when it comes to doing harm.°

First Choral Ode

The streams of sacred rivers run backwards:°   A   410
Justice and everything go in reverse;
Men's plans treacherous, faith sworn by gods
No longer fixed and secure;

---

403. *a test of courage:* another "heroic" sentiment.

404. *You mustn't be laughed at:* see note on v. 383.

405 *Sisyphian marriages:* Since Sisyphus in Greek myth was noted for deviousness and trickery (for which he was punished by being made to roll up a steep hill a boulder which he was never able to bring to the top), Medea means that Jason acted in an underhanded way in contracting his new marriage. (Some accounts made Sisyphus the founder and first king of Corinth and father of Creon; or even husband of Medea! In later times travelers were shown his tomb near Corinth.)

406. *your father (Aietes)…his father, the Sun:* generations of not only heroic but semi-divine ancestors are looking upon her to see how "nobly" Medea will respond to the challenge which she now faces.

409. An epigrammatic line which gave some grounds to those who, like Aristophanes (see *Frogs* 1044 ff.), affected to be shocked at Euripides' protrayal of women (it matches the epigrammatic vv. 263-6 above).

410-45. *First Choral Ode:* The Chorus, having taken up a formal position in the orchestra, now sing and dance to a song whose matching stanzas are a sign of correspondingly matching dance-steps to accompany the singing. Music was provided by a flute-player. The theme of the first two stanzas is odd and somewhat obscurely expressed. In the first part, the women of Corinth respond to Medea's stated intention to seek revenge by asserting that women, whose achievements have been given less than their due by male poets, will now "have renown" (v. 414), and would have had even more (although the logic of stanza A[1] is rather fuzzy) if there had been women poets, who could have reported men's misdeeds as men through the ages have women's. In stanzas B and B[1] they recapitulate some points already made: Medea's heart was maddened by love of Jason (see v. 8); she passed from the Black Sea through the "twin rocks" (see vv. 2, 210-12). She is a foreigner in Corinth (v. 222) and is being exiled (255, etc.) in dishonor (vv. 20, 33), with no father's home to return to (32-3, 166; 506 ff. below).

But the tables will turn. I'll have renown.
Honor will come° at last to the female race;   415
No longer will women be victims of bad reports.   420
The ancient songs will at last diminish   A¹
That sing of my faithlessness.
To us no talent of raising the lyre's
Heavenly voice was given   /   425
By Apollo, leader of songs. I'd have sung
A contrary hymn against the male race;
For ages can tell as much of men as of *us*.   430
Medea, you sailed from your father's home   B
With maddened heart,° and passed the twin rocks
Of the sea.° A foreign land   435
You live in. Your husband's bed
You've lost, poor woman. The land now drives you away,
A dishonored exile.
The grace of oaths is gone.° Shame° no longer   B¹
Resides in great Greece, but has flown skyward.   440
And for you no father's home
Will give shelter from sorrows. The bed
Now has another mistress standing over it,
A royal bride.   445

(Enter Jason from the western, stage-left, entrance way.)

Jason

This is not the first time° I've seen
What an irreparable evil a savage temper is.
You could have stayed in this country and this house
If you had borne more lightly the plans of your masters°;

418-20. *Honor will come:* the irony is fairly heavy-handed. Medea's honor will be redressed (see preceding note), but at what cost! And the women will continue to be "victims of bad reports," even more than before because of Medea's actions.

434. *maddened heart:* driven mad, that is by love; see note on v. 8 above.

434-5. *twin rocks Of the sea:* cf. v. 2 "Clashing rocks," with note there.

439. *The grace of oaths is gone:* because Jason has broken his oaths to Medea (v. 21-2, 162-3, 209-10).

Shame: personified, as often.

446. *not the first time:* from his first words Jason is shown up as one who is pompous and undiplomatic in manner (he will reveal himself as incredibly insensitive and opportunistic as well).

449. *If you had borne more lightly the plans of your masters:* like waving a red flag before Medea's fierce individualism.

But for your foolish words you'll be driven out, 450
It's no business of mine;° never stop
Saying that Jason is the vilest of men;
But the things that you've been saying about the rulers—
Consider it gain that you're punished only by exile.
I've always tried to smooth the ruffled temper 455
Of the princes, and I wanted you to stay!
But you don't give up your folly, continually
Carping at the rulers, so you'll be expelled.
In spite of this I haven't rejected dear ones,
But have come out of forethought for you, woman,° 460
So you won't go into exile with the children,
Penniless, destitute. Exile brings with it°
A flock of sorrows. For even though you hate me,
I could never harbor malicious thoughts against you.

Medea

Vilest of creatures!° This is the worst thing 465
I can say about your so-called manliness!
You've come to us, you, the worst enemy
Of the gods and me and the whole human race?°
This isn't being bold or even brash,
To wrong loved ones and look them in the eye, 470
But one of the worst diseases of humankind,
A lack of shame.° But you were right to come,
For when I have spilled out my abuse of you,
My heart will be lightened and your ears will burn.
    I'll begin right back at the beginning.° 475

---

451. *It's no business of mine:* but it is, or should be, even as a former husband, and one who has derived so much benefit from her.

460. *But have come…woman:* the word he uses can also signify "wife"; perhaps the irony is intended on the poet's part.

462. *Exile brings with it:* Jason's sententiousness strikes us as unfeeling, but may not have struck a Greek audience so. His offers of help seem well-intentioned enough (he may be thinking, but does not say, "What would people say if I didn't help you?")

465. *Vilest of creatures!:* a not surprising vehemence on Medea's part.

468. This line is often excised (it recurs at v. 1324): I prefer to keep it (but see note on vv. 520-1, below).

472. *A lack of shame:* as the chorus had sung in the preceding ode, "Shame no longer resides in great Greece" (vv. 439-40).

475. *I'll begin right back at the beginning:* for all the formality of the rhetoric (cf vv. 214 ff., and note on 214, *Enter Medea*), this seems vigorous and direct, and not (to my ear at least) as studied as her opening speech.

I rescued you, as the Greeks know who were
Your shipmates long ago aboard the Argo,°
When you were sent to master the monstrous bulls
With yokes and sow the furrow with seeds of death.°
The serpent who never slept, his twisted coils   480
Protecting the golden fleece, I was the one
Who killed it and held out to you a beacon of safety.
I betrayed both my father and my house°
And went with you to Pelias' land, Iolkos,
Showing in that more eagerness than sense.°   485
I put Pelias to death in the most painful way—
By his own daughters.° I destroyed his whole house
And in return for this, you foulest of men,
You betrayed us and took a new wife,
Even though you have children. Were you childless,°   490
One might forgive you this liaison. But now
The trust of oaths is gone.° I do not know
Whether you think those gods no longer rule,
And men's present laws are newly passed,°
Since you're conscious of having broken your oaths to me.   495
    Ah! You often clasped my right hand
And solemnly appealed to me to save you,

---

477. *Your shipmates...aboard the Argo:* the exploits of the Argonauts were one of the great mythic sagas; see Introduction and v. 1387.

479. *sow the furrow with seeds of death:* as noted in the Introduction, Medea's father put various obstacles in Jason's path to prevent him from getting the Golden Fleece: the fire-breathing bulls just mentioned, and these "Sown Men" which sprang from the soil into which Jason had sown the dragon's teeth. Using various of her magic devices Medea helped him overcome these obstacles.

483. *I betrayed both my father and my house:* once again she returns to the point (vv. 31-2, 166) as if it were resting heavily on her conscience; it also reminds Jason of the magnitude of her sacrifice for him—and his debt to her.

485. *more eagerness than sense:* because, for all her reputation for wisdom (vv. 285, 303), she was foolish in her trust of Jason.

485-6. *Pelias...his own daughters:* See Introduction, and note on v. 9

490. *Were you childless:* in ancient Greece concubinage was permitted, especially for purposes of producing a male heir to inherit a man's property and carry on the family name.

492. *The trust of oaths is gone,* and 495. *having broken your oaths:* cf vv. 162-3 209-10, 418 and 439 (where the language is close to Medea's here).

493-4. *those gods no longer rule...laws are newly passed:* she emphasizes that in reneging on his oath never to forsake her Jason has transgressed an age-old rule of behavior, felt to be one of the most sacrosanct in the human ethical code.

You evil man! My hopes all misfired.
    Well, then, I shall deal with you as a friend:
What good am I supposed to get from you? 500
Still, if I ask, you'll be shown up as more shameful.
Now where should I go? To my father's house?
My country which I betrayed° to come with you?
To Pelias' wretched daughters?° Of course, they'd welcome
The slayer° of their father into their home! 505
This is how things are: to my nearest and dearest
I stand hateful, and those I shouldn't have wronged
I've made into enemies by doing you a favor.
So in return for this you've made me, to many
Greek women, enviable: for I have *you*, 510
A splendid, trusted husband, for all my sorrow,
Even if I must leave this country in exile,
Without friends, my children alone and I
Alone with them; a fine blot on the new
Bridegroom's record, that both the children and I
Who saved you should wander over the earth as beggars. 515
    Zeus, why did you give to men clear signs
To distinguish counterfeit gold from true, but as for
Humans, no stamp is impressed on their bodies
By which the bogus ones can be discerned?

Chorus-Leader

A terrible thing is temper° and knows no cure 520
When dear ones wrangle and fall to fighting each other.

Jason

I must, it seems,° not fall short of perfection

502-3. *my father's house…My country which I betrayed:* cf. v. 283, with note.

504. *Pelias' wretched daughters:* cf.vv. 485-6, with note.

504-5. *They'd welcome the slayer:* Medea's heavy sarcasm turns more acid at vv. 509-10, "You've made me envied among Greeks women."

516-19. *Zeus, why did you give, etc:* the same idea is expressed in *Hippolytus* (vv. 925-31), written a few years later.

520-21. *A terrible thing is temper, etc:* the Chorus' rather bland couplet serves (as often) to mark the end of a speech by one character before the floor is turned over, so to speak, to the opponent in the debate (cf. v. 546) (It should be noted that Jason's reply of 54 lines matches Medea's preceding one of 55 almost exactly; removal of v. 468 would bring them into exact correspondence.)

522. *I must, it seems, etc:* Jason begins with a rhetorical warm-up, longer than his couplet at vv. 446-7.

In speaking, but just like an expert helmsman,
Haul up my sail and run before the storm°
Of harsh words your tongue spews, woman.   525
But since you so proudly prate about your favors,
I believe the only one of gods or mortals
Who saved me during my voyage was—Aphrodite!°
A subtle mind you have, but are very slow
To grasp the story of how Eros, Love, forced you   530
With his unerring arrows° to save my person.
Still, I don't insist on a strict accounting;
The benefits you offered have worked out well.
But what you got in return for saving me
Was far more than you gave,° as I shall prove.   535
First, instead of a barbarian land, Greece
Is your country now; you have a taste of justice
And the use of laws not subject to force.
All the Greeks can see that you are wise,°
So you have renown, but if you lived at the ends   540
Of the earth,° no one would take account of you.
For me, I wouldn't care to have gold in the house
Or a singing voice sweeter than Orpheus'°
Unless I reached some pinnacle of fame.
    So much for my own efforts—and remember,   545

523-4. *like an expert helsman…run before the storm:* although maritime imagery is frequent (see vv. 278-9, with note), it seems to me particularly frigid here.

527-8. *the only one of gods…was Aphrodite!:* a similar argument is used by Helen in the *Trojan Women* (vv. 929 ff and cf. vv. 982-9, where Hecuba retorts "Aphrodite is just a name given by humans to their lack of self-control!"), but here the sterile and ungallant remark seems intended to characterize Jason as especially unfeeling.

530-1. Love's arrows were a cliché in Greek poetry; see vv. 633-4.

534-5 *what you got…more than you gave:* Jason turns mean-spirited.

536-41. *instead of a barbarian land…a taste of justice…laws not subject to force…see that you are wise:* it seems incredible that Jason does not see how misapplied all his points are. These are hardly "benefits" (v. 533), given that Medea has, by summary decree, been stripped of her status and must leave Corinth with (as yet) no sure destination, her reputation for murderous craft preceding her. Many commentators have felt that Euripides is scoring points against his smug contemporaries. If this is the way that superior Greeks treat those less privileged, let us have "barbarian" mores every time!

540-1. *if you lived at the ends Of the earth:* as Medea has said, bitterly and often, she wishes she had never left Colchis.

543. *singing voice sweeter than Orpheus':* Orpheus' power over beasts and the natural world through his music was proverbial (the image recurs frequently in Greek poetry). The platitude makes Jason's argument sound particularly hollow.

You were the one who called for a debate.

Now for the blame° you cast at my royal match:
In this I shall prove, first, that I am wise;
Second, self-controlled; finally, your greatest friend
And the children's—wait and hear me out.°   550
When I moved my residence to here from Iolkos
(bringing along a pack of problems with no solution),°
What luckier scheme could I have found than this,
To marry the King's daughter, I, a fugitive?
Not—what's chafing you—that I hated your bed   555
And was struck by desire for a new bride,
Nor eager for a contest in child-producing;
I have enough and find no fault with them.
Uppermost in my mind was for us to live
Well-off,° not destitute, for I know   560
That an impoverished man is shunned by all his friends,
I wanted to raise the children in a manner befitting
My family,° producing brothers for those I had
With you, to bind the family together so I
Might prosper. You don't need more children,° while I   565
See the profit of benefitting those we have
With more to come. Was this a bad plan?
You'd agree, if the marriage didn't chafe you.
You women have come to such a point° that you think,

---

547. *Now for the blame, etc:* Jason apparently does not see that, so far from exonerating him, to reveal himself as thus coldly calculating in his new marriage makes our estimation of him plunge still further. His "defense" reads like a case-study in opportunistic manipulativeness.

550. *wait, and hear me out:* obviously Medea makes some kind of movement or gesture, perhaps turning away as if to leave.

552. *a pack of problems with no solution:* it is not clear what Jason is referring to beyond the fact that Medea's presence was an encumbrance to his new dynastic plans.

559-60. *for us to live Well-off:* on the surface of it, this sounds plausible enough. When, however, we consider how much Medea has sacrificed because of her single-minded passion for Jason, we see how far apart these two are (and must always have been, unless he experienced a drastic sea-change), how little such mundane considerations could ever have mattered to her.

562-3. *in a manner befitting My family:* a note of self-importance, even snobbishness on Jason's part, only latent so far, is thus explicitly struck. Note also the egoistic tone "my family" and, in 564-5, "I might prosper."

565. *You don't need more children:* can Jason have said anything more callous (and double-edged, in light of the way the plot will turn)?

569. *You women have come to such a point:* the implication is that women are narrowly focused on sex and have a romantic view of it, whereas men have a broader outlook (this is an uglier version of the kind of distinction Medea had made at vv. 238-47).

If things go right in bed, you have everything;   570
But if your sex-life is suffering, then you become
Vicious enemies of all your best and dearest.
There ought to have been some other way° for mortals
To procreate—the female race could vanish!
Then, men wouldn't have had this misery.   575

Chorus-Leader

Jason, you've packaged these arguments attractively;
Still—though you may not want to hear it—I think
You're acting against justice° in betraying your wife.

Medea

How different I am from the rest of the human race!
For me, the man who is a villain, but clever   580
In speech, would have to pay the highest fine;
Confident of cloaking his villainy in fine words,
He dares *anything*; still, he's not over-wise.
So stop putting a false face before me
With slippery words; one line'll lay you flat°:   585
If you hadn't been evil you would have persuaded me first,
Then got married, not kept it quiet from dear ones.

Jason

And you, I suppose, would then have furthered that plan
Had I mentioned the marriage, when, even now,
You dare not eject the great rancor from your heart.   590

Medea

That wasn't the reason; it would've looked bad
For you to be growing old with a foreign wife.

Jason

No, I assure you, it was not for a woman's sake
That I undertook my present royal marriage,
But, as I've already told you, because I wanted   595
To rescue you and produce princely brothers
To help my children, a prop to support the house.

---

573. *There ought to have been some other way:* Hippolytus makes a similar suggestion: men should
     have been able to "deposit a weight of gold, or iron, or bronze in one of Zeus' temples and
     then go around to collect 'a seed of children' of equivalent value" (*Hippolytus* 616-24; he
     doesn't say by what method the seed would grow).

578. *You're acting against justice:* this puts the charge against him in most explicit terms (see also
     above, vv. 209-10, with note).

585. *lay you flat:* a wrestling metaphor.

Medea

> I want no share in a "happy" life that grieves me,
> Or "prosperity" that chafes against my heart.

Jason

> You know how to change your prayer and appear wiser?   600
> Pray that good never appear to you "grievous,"
> Nor think that you're "unlucky" when you're not.

Medea

> Go on, insult me! You have somewhere to turn;
> I shall leave this country in exile, alone.°

Jason

> You chose it yourself! Don't blame anyone else!   605

Medea

> By marrying someone else?° Forsaking you?

Jason

> By casting impious curses against the rulers.

Medea

> Yes, and I could be a curse° to your family, too!

Jason

> I don't intend to debate with you any further.
> But if you wish° me to give you or the children   610
> Extra money for your trip into exile, tell me;
> I'm ready to give it with a lavish hand,
> And write to foreign friends who will help you out.
> You'd be foolish not to take up this offer, woman;
> You'll profit more by getting rid of your anger.   615

Medea

> I wouldn't have any dealings with *your* friends,
> Nor take what *you* gave; don't bother offering.
> "The gifts of an evil giver bring no gain."

---

604. *I shall leave this country…alone*: she returns to an earlier theme.

606. *By marrying someone else?*: it is biting sarcasm, an effective thrust at Jason.

608. *I could be a curse*: a covert warning that she will not take the insult (v. 603) lying down.

610-14. *if you wish, etc*: Jason is careful to preserve the proprieties, but this is a mere token: let it not be said that he is the kind of man who does not pay alimony and child-support.

Jason

I call upon the gods to witness° that I
Was willing to do anything for you and the children;   620
But you reject favors, stubbornly cast
Your dear ones away; you'll suffer the more for it.

Medea

Go away. Desire for your new bride
Overwhelms you, who've been so long away from home!
Marry! Perhaps, if God supports my words,   625
You've made a match you'll one day have cause to lament.°

Second Choral Ode°

When the Loves° descend in full force they never enhance   A
Men's fame or virtue, but if Aphrodite approaches   630
With reserve, there is no more gracious goddess.
Mistress, never use me as a target, shooting golden arrows
Tipped with desire, unerring in aim.

Lady Restraint, befriend me (for it is the gods' greatest gift).   A¹
May Aphrodite never drive me to fight with my husband,
Striking my spirit with love of another man,   640

---

619. *I call upon the gods to witness:* Jason is being legalistically (and moralistically) correct; ritually and juridically, at least, his "hands are clean."

626. *cause to lament:* I translate E.R. Dodds' conjecture, accepted by Diggle, for the manuscript-reading "renounce."

627-62. *Second Choral Ode:* In the first half, the Chorus sing of the dangers of love when it goes to extremes (there is an ode on a similar theme in Sophocles' *Antigone*, vv. 781-800); in the second half they return to the topic of exile and end with more general commiseration for Medea. The theme of "moderation in love" seems at first sight rather straightforward, but as applied to Medea's and Jason's situation it is not. So far from being immoderate, Jason seems incapable of loving at all (we have just heard him say that his new marriage is not due to infatuation, but a coolly calculated match of convenience (vv. 555 ff.) As for Medea, her uncontrolled passion for Jason is a thing of the past (vv. 8, 228, 526 ff.). And "never drive me to fight with my husband" (vv. 638-9) comes in rather oddly, considering that we have just witnessed a fight between Medea and Jason, but not one resulting from the fact that either one (unless Jason is dissembling) has "fallen in love" with someone else.

629. *Loves,* more familiar to us as "Cupids," are Aphrodite's agents; the violence of their activity here is in contrast with the peaceful picture at vv. 835 ff.

Two other themes touched in the Chorus are of more general relevance to the drama, "Lady Restraint" (*Sophrosune,* personified, 635) and "men's fame" (630; cf. 414, "I'll have renown"). Both of these have an indirect and negative application to Medea: her revenge, motivated as it is by perverted passion, will fly in the face of the Chorus' praises of "Restraint," and will bring her a kind of fame, but hardly one to be envied.

But do me the honor of making my marriage peaceful,°
And decide shrewdly about women's loves.

My city, my home! I pray   B   645
Never to go into exile,
Never to lead that kind of life
of endless, unmanageable suffering.
Die! To die would be better,   650
and bring my life's day to an end forever.
No pain is worse than to lose one's country.

We saw, we don't have to take   B¹
Another's word, Medea: 655
No city, no friend pitied your pain,
the worst of sufferings.
Perish unloved the one
who does not unlock a pure heart to friends;   660
No friend of mind will he ever be.

(Enter Aigeus, King of Athens.) °

Aigeus

Medea, I wish you well. No one knows
How to address a better greeting to friends.

Medea

Greetings to you, too, Aigeus,° wise Pandion's   665
Son. From where are you coming to this land?

Aigeus

I've come from Delphi,° Apollo's ancient oracle.

641-2. The poet's meaning is unclear; I have translated what I think he meant to say.

663. *(Enter Aigeus....)*. This renowned Athenian king comes in along the eastern, stage-right, entranceway. His appearance is unexpected. He comes just in the nick of time for, as Medea had said (vv. 289-91), she is in need of some "tower of refuge" in order to proceed with her revenge-plot. (Some critics have objected that his appearance is unmotivated, and a bit too convenient for the plot. But it has also been pointed out that the "children theme," especially as it ironically applies to Medea—she is willing to help Aigeus attain his desire for children, while at the same time contemplating the murder of her own—provides some continuity with the rest of the play.)

665. *Greetings to you, too, Aigeus:* it is most unusual for a newcomer to appear without being announced and without identifying him- or herself. How does Medea know who it is? Her supernatural powers? (Or a slip by the poet?)

667. *I've come from Delphi:* a return journey from Delphi to Athens would not pass near Corinth; Aigeus has detoured for a special reason (vv. 682 ff.).

Medea

What took you to the earth's center of prophecy?

Aigeus

To find out how I might become a father.

Medea

By heavens! You're childless at your time of life?   670

Aigeus

Childless, indeed, by some cruel stroke of fate.

Medea

You're married?° You've had experience with women?

Aigeus

Indeed, it's not for lack of a wife or marriage.

Medea

What did Apollo tell you about children?   675

Aigeus

Words too wise for a man to understand.

Medea

Is it right for me to know the god's response?

Aigeus

Certainly, for a clever mind indeed° is needed.

Medea

What did he say, then? Speak, if it is allowed.

Aigeus

Not to release the wine-skin's hanging neck°—

Medea

Until you do what, come to what place?   680

Aigeus

Until I come to my father's hearth once more.

Medea

But why, then, have you put your ship in *here*?

---

672. *You're married?:* Medea is methodical, almost clinical, in her approach to Aigeus' problem (an ancient note informs us that Aigeus had in fact had two wives).

677. *a clever mind indeed:* Jason had mentioned Medea's international reputation (v. 539).

679. *release the wine-skin's hanging neck:* this was interpreted in antiquity to mean "have sexual intercourse"; no doubt rightly.

Aigeus

There is a man named Pittheus, ruler of Trozen°—

Medea

Most pious son of Pelops, as they say.

Aigeus

I want to share the prophecy with him.   685

Medea

Yes, for he is wise and has much experience.

Aigeus

And the dearest of my military comrades.

Medea

I wish you well; good luck in what you're after—

(Looks at her closely)

Aigeus

Your eyes are moist,° your face is streaked with tears....

Medea

Aigeus, my husband is the worst man in the world!   690

Aigeus

What's wrong? Be clearer about what's troubling you.

Medea

Jason is wronging me; I've done nothing to *him*.

Aigeus

Wronging you how? Tell it to me more clearly.

Medea

He's taken another as mistress of his home.

Aigeus

You mean he's dared to do such a vile thing?   695

Medea

He has. His former "dear ones" are now dishonored.

---

683. *Pittheus...Trozen:* Trozen was southeast of Corinth, in the area known as the "Argolid." It is Pittheus' daughter, Aithra, whom Aigeus will impregnate, thus becoming the father of Theseus (for Theseus' importance in Medea's future life at Athens, see Introduction).

689. *Your eyes are moist:* since the Greek actors' faces were masked, no obvious tears would have been visible. Medea probably puts her hands to her face, or attempts to cover it with her cloak, thus prompting Aigeus' question.

Aigeus

Was it love? Or did his marriage with you turn sour?

Medea

A "great" love,° and breach of faith with us.

Aigeus

Forget it, then, if he's as bad as you say.

Medea

He fell in love with a marriage-bond with kings.   700

Aigeus

Who's making the match for him? Finish your story.

Medea

Creon, the man who rules this land of Corinth.

Aigeus

You're right then to feel aggrieved, Medea.

Medea

I'm lost! What's more, I'm driven into exile.

Aigeus

By whom? You mention now a new injury!   705

Medea

Creon it is who's driving me out of Corinth.

Aigeus

And Jason allows it? I don't approve of that!

Medea

He says he doesn't, but must "put up" with it—
I implore you solemnly, appealing by your beard°
And knees, and make myself your suppliant: 710
Have pity, have pity on me in my misfortune;
Don't allow them to drive me out, solitary,
But take me into your country and your home.
May the gods fulfill what you desire of them,
Children, and may you achieve a happy death.   715
You don't know what a lucky find this is!

---

698. *a "great" love:* we know that Medea is being sarcastic in light of Jason's explanation at vv. 555 ff. and 593-4; she explains her meaning to Aigeus at v. 700.

709-10. *appealing by your beard, etc:* a most solemn form of supplication; Medea had said something similar to Creon (v. 324), equally effectively.

For I can end your childlessness and make you
Able to father children: I have magic° for this.

Aigeus

For many reasons, Medea, I am eager
To grant you this favor: first, the gods°;   720
Then, for the sake of the children that you've promised—
For I am obsessed with the desire to be a father.
So be it, then. If you come to my country
I shall try to protect you, as I agreed.
But I tell you one thing in advance, Medea—   725
I'm not willing to escort you from this land;°
But if you come to my place on your own,
You'll stay there unharmed; I shall not surrender you.
But secure your removal from this land yourself.
For I wish to incur no blame, even from strangers.°   730

Medea

I accept the terms. Your faithfulness° to your promise
Is all the benefit I need of you.

Aigeus

Surely you trust me? What's troubling you?

Medea

I do trust you. But Pelias' house and Creon
Are my enemies. If they try to drag me away,   735
Your oath will keep you from giving me up.
If you just promise and don't swear by the gods,

717-18. *I can end your childlessness…I have magic:* it is unusual, and bold, for Medea to advertise her magic powers in this way (but cf. vv. 384-5 and 789 below); this is the "witch" in her speaking.

720. *first, the gods:* Aigeus has recognized the validity of Medea's complaints (vv. 703 ff.) and she has become his suppliant (vv. 709-10), so he feels he has a moral duty to her. At the human level, too, as he admits (vv. 711-12), he has a powerful motive for enlisting her help.

725-31. I follow the traditional order of lines as they appear in most manuscripts. Diggle suppresses 725-6 and rearranges as follows 729-727-728-730, the scheme of one papyrus (but with this order the explanatory "*for* I wish to incur no blame," v. 730, remains unmotivated).

726. *I'm not willing to escort you from this land:* he probably feels that to do so might involve him in animosity with Corinth's rulers. More likely, however, the point is introduced to provide an excuse for Medea to show her self-reliance and arrange a spectacular exit on her own.

731. *Your faithfulness:* once burnt (by Jason), twice shy. The plot takes an interesting detour to prolong the scene and also, incidentally, demonstrate Medea's hard-nosed practicality.

You might become their friend; a summons from them
Might make you yield, for my claims are weak,
Whereas *they* have both wealth and royal power.   740

Aigeus

I well understand why you're making this request.
If you wish, I do not refuse to take an oath:
It will mean greater safety for me, to have
Something to show your enemies as a plea,
And it makes your case more secure. Name your gods.°   745

Medea

Swear by the soil of Earth and Sun, the father
Of my father, and add the rest of the race of gods.

Aigeus

To do or not do what? Speak further.

Medea

Never to drive me out of your land yourself,°
Or, if an enemy wants to take me off,   750
Not to allow it willingly while you live.

Aigeus

I swear by Earth, the holy light of the Sun,
And all the gods, to abide by what you say.

Medea

Enough. And to suffer what if you do not abide?

Aigeus

The sort of things that happen to impious men.   755

Medea

Farewell, go on your way. All is well.
I shall come to your city by the quickest means
When I've done what I intend° and got what I wish.

---

745. *Name your gods:* a standard procedure in oath-taking. The solemnity of the undertaking
   is enhanced and Medea gets a chance to refer to her illustrious divine ancestry (vv. 746-7).

749. *Never to drive me out of your land yourself:* as noted in the Introduction, Medea's life at
   Athens was to be anything but smooth; in fact, since Aigeus later expelled her from Athens
   for trying to poison Theseus, he, like Jason, became an oath-breaker.

758. *When I've done what I intend:* an ominous hint of what is to follow.

Chorus *(to Aigeus)*

> May Lord Hermes Escorter°
> Bring you home, and may you accomplish   760
> What you eagerly hope to obtain;
> For you are a noble man, Aigeus,
> As far as I can judge.

(Exit Aigeus.)

Medea

> O Zeus and Justice of Zeus and light of the Sun!°
> *(to chorus)* Now, my friends, sweet victory over enemies   765
> Will be mine! I've set out along the road!
> Now there's hope of paying out my enemies!
> The one thing missing this man has provided:
> A safe harbor after our plans are achieved.
> I'll make fast my mooring line° to him   770
> When I come to Athena's town and citadel.
>   Now I shall tell you exactly what I'm planning;
> You'll hear, but not rejoice at what I say.
> I'll send one from among my servants to Jason
> And ask that he come to see me face-to-face,   775
> And when he comes, I'll speak soft words to him—
> I agree to what he wants and think it fine
> For him to give me up and marry a princess,
> A suitable plan and well devised by him.
> I'll beg him for my children to remain   780
> Not because I want to leave my sons
> In a hostile land for enemies to insult,

---

759. *Hermes Escorter:* one of the standard epithets of the gods' messenger (especially as escorter of dead souls to the underworld).

764 ff. With Aigeus' solemn promise to give her asylum, if she can get to Athens herself, the missing link in Medea's intended chain of vengeance has been forged and put in place. Success is now at last within her grasp and she allows herself to gloat as she works out details of her murderous plan and begins to savor the evil fruits of success.

764. *O Zeus and Justice of Zeus and light of the Sun:* solemn prayers of this kind usually involved naming three divinities—Zeus is summoned as supreme Olympian (see vv. 169, with note; 332). Justice, sometimes personified as Zeus' daughter, means for Medea simply vengeance on those who have wronged her (she had called on justice under the name of Themis earlier, v. 160; and cf. vv. 209-10, 578 and below 1389, when it will be Jason's turn). The sun is the purest and most powerful of natural elements, as well as her grandfather. The prayer sounds (and is meant to sound) almost sacrilegious.

770. *make fast my mooring line:* a nautical image; cf. vv. 278-9 with note, 523-4.

But merely to snare and kill the king's daughter.
The children I'll send off to the bride with gifts
In their hands, asking not to go into exile—   785
A fine-textured robe and a golden garland;
And if she takes the adornment and puts it on,
She and all who touch the girl will die:
Such is the poison° with which I'll anoint the gifts.
There, I'm finished with that part of the plot, but—   790

(she groans)

I moan for the kind of task that I must proceed
To accomplish.° For I shall put the children to death°—
My children. No one will save them from me.
When I have utterly ruined all Jason's house,
I shall leave the country, accused of my dear children's   795
Murder, and having dared the unholiest of deeds.

(to Chorus)

For to be laughed at by enemies° is intolerable, friends.

---

782. Diggle follows Brunck in deleting this verse on the basis of its similarity to vv. 1060-1 below, but I feel this is unnecessary (I likewise retain 785).

789. *Such is the poison:* Medea's magic powers were hinted at in the matter of Pelias' daughters (vv. 386-7, 504-5) and alluded to by her openly when she promised to help Aigeus overcome his sterility (v. 718). Here the full range of her magic is revealed: she has preparations which render garments incendiary when they come in contact with the skin, and to which anyone who touches them will adhere (see vv. 1212 ff. below).

791-2. *the kind of task...To accomplish:* she uses "heroic" language; to overcome her natural sympathies as a mother and kill her children will require a perverted kind of bravery.

792. *I shall put the children to death:* critics vary in their opinions about when exactly Medea decides to kill her children. My personal view is that, although the idea may have been circling around in her subconscious for some time—see, for example, the Nurse's bald statement, "she hates her children" (v. 36) and Medea's own words at vv. 112-3—it is only now that she finally determines actually to put them to death. She might, after all, have arranged to kill Jason—threats against her husband were common knowledge (v. 288)—and perhaps also the bride and her father, but she now hits upon a truly fiendish form of revenge: Jason's dynastic plans, at least as regards his children by her, will be thwarted, and she will wound him most painfully by using the considerable love which she knows he feels for their sons (see the section beginning with v. 1303 below). But at what cost to herself! It is not a casual decision, and she will several times come close to abandoning her resolve (see vv. 1040 and following, below).

797. *to be laughed at by enemies:* as already noted (vv. 383 with note, 404; and cf. below v. 1049), it was a characteristic of the ancient Greeks (especially males) to avoid anything that might contribute to loss-of-face.

So—what profit for me in living?° who have
No country, no home, no shelter from misfortune.
I made a mistake *then* in leaving the house   800
Of my father and putting faith in a *Greek* man's°
Words; I'll punish him,° with God's help.
The children he had by me he'll never see
Alive, and those he hopes for by his new bride
He'll not be able to beget, for she is evil   805
And evil must her death be by my poisons.
Let no one think of me as "poor" or "weak"
Or "retiring", but quite the contrary, a millstone
Around my enemies' necks, a boon to my friends.
The lives of people like that are most renowned.°   810

Chorus Leader

You shared your innermost thoughts with us, and so,
Wishing as much to support society's laws
As to aid you, I tell you to give up your plan.°

Medea

It cannot be otherwise. I understand why you speak
Thus; you were not mistreated, as I was.   815

Chorus Leader

But how will you dare to kill your offspring, woman?

Medea

Because it is this that will sting my man most.

---

798. *what profit for me in living:* life has lost its meaning to her, or, less probably, she might even be fleetingly thinking of suicide. (I do not accept Diggle's deletion of vv. 798-9, following Leo.)

801. *a Greek man's:* this is her retort to Jason's absurd claims that he benefitted her in bringing her to Greece (vv. 536-7).

799-802. *who have no country...I made a mistake...I'll punish him:* she returns to these well-worn themes of what she has "sacrificed," perhaps to confirm her resolve to seek such terrible retribution from the one whom she holds responsible.

810. *The lives of people like that are most renowned:* Medea once again projects herself into a vanished heroic past; what she forgets is that these heroes' actions in sacrificing everything to their self-esteem (cf. Achilles) often brought misery to those around them and sometimes death to themselves (cf. Ajax).

813. *I tell you to give up your plan:* their opposition had been foreseen by Medea (v. 773), but this must strike us as a weak response to Medea's statement that she intends to murder the princess and whoever touches her, and then commit infanticide. (Euripides is prepared to sacrifice realism here. They will not intervene, because the plot require that they should not, so why even try?)

Chorus Leader

You'll only end up being the most miserable of women.°

Medea

So be it. From now on your speech is superfluous.

Go, you *(to the nurse)*, and bring Jason to me—   820
For I entrust to you all important tasks—
Tell him nothing of what I've decided to do,
If you wish your mistress well, and are a woman.°

Third Choral Ode°

The Athenians, Erechtheus' sons,° have long been blessed;   A
The gods' own children they are,   825
And sprung from a sacred land that no invader
Has ever despoiled.°
They browse long among thoughts°
Sage and famous;
Treading always delicately through   830
Crystalline air°

---

818. *the most miserable of women:* this puts "Everyperson's" case most clearly. No normal woman would act thus, for the prospect of such great remorse would forestall her. Medea is extraordinary—beyond comprehension—even in this, her ability to suppress "normal" humans instincts of motherhood.

823. *and are a woman:* Medea had similarly appealed to the female instincts of the Chorus at vv. 407-8 above.

Third Choral Ode (824-865) The first part of the song is mainly a hymn of praise to Athens, the gentle beauty of its landscape and its humane virtues; in short, its civilization (a not inappropriate theme to present to an audience which was to face war with Sparta within months). It is a shocking contradiction for so glorious a city to provide shelter to one who could contemplate such a heinous crime. In the last stanza they at last give voice to their horror and disbelief at what she intends (see note on v. 813 above).

824 *Erechtheus' sons:* Erechtheus was an early king of Athens. The Athenians were often referred to as his descendants (see next note).

826-7. *sprung from a sacred land that no invader Has ever despoiled:* it was a constant boast by the Athenians, made even by Thucydides, that their country had never been subject to immigration or invasion from abroad. According to their nationalistic mythology, they were descended from Erichthonios (often confused or identified with Erechtheus), who was the son of Hephaestus and Gaia, mother Earth. So they were literally indigenous, native sons!

828. *They browse long among thoughts:* Athenians also liked to think of themselves as having long traditions of indigenous poetry and philosophy; in fact, before 500 B.C. Athens had little native talent of this type and even after, many philosophers and literary persons who practiced there were foreigners.

830-1. *through Crystalline air:* the bright violet-hued atmosphere of Athens was renowned, and often served as a theme for poetry.

Where once, it is said, the Holy Nine,
Pieria's Muses,° created
Harmony,° the golden-haired.

They celebrate in song how Aphrodite,°   A¹   835
Drawing water at fair-flowing Cephisus'° streams,
Sent moderate breezes sweetly blowing
Over the land;
How she always puts on her hair   840
A fragrant garland of roses
And sends the Loves° to be
Wisdom's partners,°
To share all her manifold tasks
And bring forth with her
Virtue of every kind.   845

How, then, can a city   B
Of sacred rivers,
One that welcomes friends,
Receive you, a child-slayer,
The unholy inhabitant?°   850
Consider the stroke at your young,
Consider the killing you plan!
We all beseech you,
Beg you in every way,
Do not slay your children.   855

Where will you get the nerve,   B¹
The heart of steel°
That can bring you

833. *Pieria's Muses:* Pieria in southern Macedonia (north of Mt Olympus) was the site of an important cult of the Muses and according to some accounts they were born there.

833-4. *Muses, created Harmony:* the Greek is ambiguous, and some have understood it in the opposite sense, "Harmony gave birth to the Muses." The Greek word-order favors the interpretation given, which is Page's. (The meaning is in any case metaphorical, for the standard genealogies of both the Muses and Harmony were quite different.)

835-41. *Aphrodite...sends the Loves:* a much prettier and less threatening picture than at vv. 629 ff.

836. *Cephisus:* with the Ilissus, one of the two major rivers of Athens.

842. *Wisdom's partners:* Wisdom is personified as a goddess, as often.

850. *inhabitant:* I translate Lueck's conjecture, accepted by Diggle; the manuscripts have "among others."

857. *heart of steel:* the text is defective here and my translation is makeshift.

To such a deed of terrible daring?
When your eyes gaze° on the children,   860
How will you hold back tears
For their slaying? You won't be able,
When the children beg
At your knees, to dip your hand
Boldly in their blood.   865

(Enter Jason.)

Jason

I've come as bidden. For all your ill-will I couldn't
Refuse you this at least, but let me hear
What new request you have to make of me.

Medea

Jason, I'm asking you to forgive the things
I said before; it's natural that you should put up   870
With my moods, for the many intimacies we shared.
I started to go over it all in my mind
And rebuked myself: "Wretched woman, why
Do I rage and rail at those who plan well?
I shall only incur the wrath of the land's rulers   875
And my husband, who is doing his very best for us
By making a royal marriage and fathering kin
For my children. Should I not put aside
My anger? What's the matter? The gods are good.
Don't I have children? Don't I know that we   880
Were outcasts from Thessaly and had no friends?"°
I thought this over and saw how very stupid
I'd been, how foolish the anger that filled me.
But now I praise you and think you were self-controlled°

---

860. *When your eyes gaze:* a very touching picture, full of poignant emotion (see note on v. 101). To this kind of appeal Medea seems to be impervious.

873-81. *"Wretched woman...had no friends?":* this remarkable monologue, in a long tradition of such lively addresses to oneself, serves a double purpose: it takes Jason off his guard (as intended), but also ironically shows us the kind of "normal" woman Medea might have been. For the position she voices here is one which any ordinary Greek woman would probably have adopted under the circumstances, realistically assessing her resources, and making the best of what she had. Medea's matter-of-fact tone reminds us how extraordinary a person she is.

884. *"Self-control" (sophron):* Medea echoes a word which Jason had primly used of himself (v. 549; it is the same root as the personified "Restraint," moderation, of v. 636). She uses the antonym, *a-phron*, in 885, which could be rendered "loss of self-control." (The irony is that, in manipulating her husband, she is totally in control of her amorous self, in contrast with the early days when he had "swept her away".)

To take on this marriage for us; it was I who lost   885
My control, when I ought rather to have joined in the scheme°
And helped bring it off, to have stood by the bed,
And taken pleasure in welcoming your new bride.
But we are what we are—I won't say that we're bad—
We women°; so you mustn't be bad just to get even   890
With us, nor oppose us with folly for folly.
I ask your forgiveness. I admit I was stupid
Then, but now I've changed my plans for the better.
O children, children, come here, come out,
Come out of the house, embrace your father.   895
Talk to him with me; *(children enter with Tutor)*

                                    lay aside with your mother

The anger we bore him. Let us be friends.

(children embrace Jason)

A truce has been called. Our anger is all gone.
Take my right hand in yours. *(aside)* The harm!
I'm thinking about the harm that still lies hidden!   900

(The children gather round and embrace her)

My dears, will you reach out your arms like this
When you have lived a long life?° Oh miserable!
I'm on the verge of tears and full of terror.
The long-standing quarrel with your father is over;
Now tears are rolling down your tender cheeks.°   905

Chorus

From my eyes, too, fresh tears spring.
I hope the harm proceeds no further° than now.

---

886. *I ought rather to have joined in the scheme, etc.:* she is, to our way of thinking, laying it on
    a bit thickly, perhaps to show up Jason's obtuseness.

889-90. *We are what we are…women:* once again Medea plays on the dependent position of
    women; see vv. 407-9 and 823 with note. Her aside, "I won't say that we're bad," seems
    on the surface at least to conflict with her earlier statement at vv. 408-9.

902. *When you have lived a long life:* her words strike a particularly pathetic note in view of her
    plan to kill them (or her resolution may be slightly faltering).

905. *your tender cheeks:* the Greek text leaves open whose cheeks are being referred to, and some
    have interpreted them as Medea's own but, as Page remarks, "Medea could not refer [thus]
    to her own appearance…at such a moment."

907. *I hope the harm proceeds no farther:* an ominously muted statement, in view of their knowl-
    edge of Medea's intentions.

Jason

I find no fault with your actions now, or then:
For it's natural that the woman-species get angry
When husbands import new brides° in beside them.   910
But your heart has now taken a turn for the better.
You've recognized, at long last, the winning plan—
The thing a woman of self-control° would do.

(He addresses the children.)

For you, boys, your father has carefully arranged
A plan that will bring safety, with the gods' help.   915
I think you'll hold first place in Corinth
With your brothers, the ones who are still to come.
Just grow up strong—the rest your father will manage,
And whichever of the gods is on our side.°
I want to see you° grow up big and strong,   920
And gain the upper hand over my enemies.

(Medea breaks down and weeps; Jason turns to her)

And you, why do you turn your fair cheek
Away? Why shed such abundant tears?
Were you not pleased to hear what I just said?

Medea

It's nothing. I was thinking about these children.   925

Jason

Cheer up, then, for I'll take good care of them.

Medea

Very well, then, I don't distrust your words;
But a woman is womanish° and prone to tears.

Jason

I don't understand why you're weeping so much for these children.

---

910. *import new brides:* a commercial metaphor.

913. *A woman of self-control:* see note on v. 884.

915-919. *with the gods' help....whichever of the gods is on our side:* is this just conventional piety on Jason's part, or is it meant to show some lingering fear, as he deals with a woman such as he knows Medea to be? (In any case, as it turns out, her powerful malevolence will overcome any help the traditional gods might have offered him).

920-1. *I want to see you...:* a standard piece of "tragic" irony, in light of the sequel (among his "enemies" [v. 921], of course, first and foremost stands Medea).

928. *a woman is womanish:* here the thought seems perfectly straightfoward and, from Medea, ironic; she is being her "natural" self.

Medea

> I bore them! When you were praying that they live, 930
> Pity came over me whether this would happen.
>
> *(She pulls herself together.)*
>
> Still, the reasons why I wanted you to come,
> Some I've already mentioned, here are the rest.
> The rulers have decided to send me from the country.
> (And it's best for me, too, I know it well, 935
> Not to be in your way or those in authority
> Here; I am thought of as the family enemy.)
> All right, then, I'll go from this land into exile,
> But in order that you bring up the children yourself,°
> Ask Creon that they not go into exile. 940

Jason

> I don't know if he'll listen, but I'll try.

Medea

> Instruct the woman you married, then, to beg
> Her father not to drive them into exile.

Jason

> Yes, and I expect she *will* persuade him,
> Especially if she's a woman like the rest.° 945

Medea

> I, too, will join with you in this task:°
> I'll send her gifts by far the most beautiful
> Now in existence, of this I'm quite certain; 948
> The children will take them.
>
> *(She turns to the servants.)*
>
> Go, tell an attendant 950
> To bring the outfit here as quickly as possible.
> She'll think herself lucky, not once but a thousand times,

---

939. *that you bring up the children yourself:* a master-stroke by Medea: she appeals to his fatherly instincts. It also serves as a prelude, an excuse for her use of the boys as intermediaries in taking the gifts to the princess.

945. *if she's a woman like the rest:* I follow Diggle in assigning this line to Jason, with the preceding, but in some manuscripts it is given to Medea. If it is spoken by Jason, it once again shows him ready to think in stereotypes.

946. *join...in this task:* she uses a "heroic" turn-of-phrase; see vv. 791-2.

949. This line has been omitted from the translation; it is repeated from 786, "a fine textured robe and a golden garland."

For having got as her bedmate the best of men,
And getting besides adornments which the Sun-god,
My father's father, gave to his descendants.   955

(A servant brings out a chest.)

Take these wedding gifts in your hands, children;
Give them to the lucky royal bride,
Her dowry—gifts in no way to be despised.

Jason

But why, foolish woman, deprive yourself of them?
Do you think the royal house lacks robes,   960
Or gold? Keep them, don't give these things away.
For if the woman thinks me worth anything°
She will place me above wealth, I am certain.

Medea

I disagree; even gods have their price,° they say,
And gold for men is worth a thousand words.   965
The spirit of luck is with her, God makes her fortune
Grow. She is young, and a princess. To spare my children
Exile, I'd give life,° not only gold.
Go children, to her father's wealthy home
And supplicate the young wife, my mistress;°   970
Beg her not to exile you from the land.
Give her this finery, and be especially careful
That she take the gifts in her hands herself.
     Go, quickly. Bring the news to your mother
That you have succeeded in what she longs to obtain.°   975

(Exit all except Medea and Chorus)

Fourth Choral Ode°

No hope remains, no hope at all,   A
That the children can live; they have gone to their deaths.

---

962. *For if the woman thinks me worth anything:* in Jason's own mind, of course, there is no
    doubt, for he is sure that he is "beyond price" in his new bride's eyes.

964. *even gods have their price:* a proverb.

968. *I'd give life:* whose life? The ambiguity is perhaps calculated.

970. *my mistress:* a new—and false—note of submissiveness on Medea's part.

975. *in what she longs to obtain:* ominous, as often with closing lines in this type of scene.

Fourth Choral Ode (976-1001) Now that Medea's evil plan seems to be going forward, the chorus
    heighten the emotions of horror and revulsion at the impending crime. They picture, first,
    Creon's daughter as she is about to put on the beautiful but deadly gifts; next, they lament
    the disaster which, in entering this marriage, Jason has brought on Corinth's royal family, as

The bride will receive a crown of gold,
A crown of death—poor girl—
Around her golden hair will place Hell's
Own jewel, with her own hands.   980

The lovely immortal gleam will persuade her   A¹
To put on the robe and golden crown;
A bride she will be among the dead.   985
Into such a trap she will fall
. Into such a deadly fate—poor girl—for death
She will no way escape.

Poor man! Cursed bridegroom of princes!   B   990
You don't realize
You're bringing destruction to your children,
And hateful death to your wife.
Poor wretch, how blind you are to your fate.   995

I lament next your grief, poor mother of children   B¹
Whom you're killing
Because of your husband's bride,
Children he lawlessly left   1000
To marry another bride.

(Children and Tutor enter)

Tutor

Madam, the children do not have to go into exile;
The royal bride gladly took the gifts
In her hands;° there's peace, now, with her and the children.

(He looks at her directly)

Why are you so disturbed when you've succeeded?   1005

---

well as on his own sons. Finally, they express sympathy for Medea and for the pain and sorrow
which they imagine await her if she indeed proceeds with the killing of her children.

From a moral point of view what follows is the central scene in the play. There is still a chance
that, even after killing the princess, Medea will not go through with her plan to murder
her sons. The dramatist shows great skill not only in keeping us in suspense until the last
possible moment, but in plumbing the depths of a mother's agonized soul as she makes and
unmakes her resolve to commit this unthinkable crime.

1003-4. *took the gifts In her hands:* just as Medea had instructed the children (vv. 972-3).

Medea

Ah....

Tutor

A cry like that does not conform to my news.   1008

Medea

I cry aloud again.

Tutor

               Does my news mean
Something I'm not aware of, something bad?   1010

Medea

You've brought the news you've brought. I don't blame you.

Tutor

Why, then, is your gaze downcast and weeping?

Medea

I've good reason to be, old man. These things
The gods and I have done,° malevolently.

Tutor

Take heart, you'll journey back with the children's help.   1015

Medea

Ah! Others I'll send on a journey first.°

Tutor

You're not the only woman to lose her children.
A human must try to bear misfortune° lightly.

Medea

I'll do as you say.° But go inside the house

1006-7. These line have been omitted from the translation, for they duplicate vv. 923-4, where they seem far more suitable.

1013-4. *These things The gods and I have done:* why does Medea bring the gods in to explain her action? Is it just a manner of speaking, or does she perhaps believe that there is a destiny that the Corinthian royal house, Jason, her children, and she herself are fulfilling?

1015, 16. *you'll journey back...send on a journey first:* the translation does not catch the important ambiguity in the Greek verbs with prefix *kat-*, which denotes both "down" and "return." The words can mean, "come from exile," or (the sense Medea uses) "send down (to Hades)."

1018. *a human must try to bear misfortune:* this maxim, or variant, is very frequently found in Greek thought.

1019. *I'll do as you say:* once again, Medea's words are ambiguous. Does she mean simply to dismiss the Tutor's sententiousness, "I know; I'll try (to bear my fate lightly)", or is the accent rather on *lightly*: Medea has, as she thinks, devised a diabolical means of escape from her misfortunes?

And see that the children get whatever they need. 1020

(Tutor exits)

Ah, children, children, you'll have a city
And home in which you'll live,° deprived of me,
Your mother, whom you'll leave behind in her misery,
But I shall go to another land, an exile;
Without the pleasure of seeing you prosperous, 1025
Without arranging a marriage,° decking the bed,
Holding the wedding torch as a mother should.
O, miserable I am for my inflexible will.°
For nothing, then, my children, I tended you,
For nothing I labored and wore myself down with toil, 1030
Enduring harsh labor-pains at your births.
Oh, the hopes I had once for you
Were many—that you would keep me in old age°
And, when I died, deck me out properly,
A sight for men to envy. Now, it's gone, 1035
That sweet concern. Without the two of you
I shall drag out a grievous and painful life.
And you will never again see with your dear eyes
Your mother° in this life, when your life has changed.
O God! Why do you turn your eyes to me, 1040
Children? Why smile this final smile?
Ahh…. What should I do? I have no heart,

1021-2. *a city And home in which you'll live:* some critics see this as having a sinister implication, "dwelling-place in the Underworld."

1026. *Without arranging a marriage:* this was a commonplace of mothers who were about to die; Alcestis on her deathbed speaks thus to her children (*Alcestis* 317-9). The interesting thing about the present passage is that the clichés would naturally be taken to mean "the children will be without their mother" (see v. 1022, "deprived of me"), but they take on a horrible hidden meaning when we realize that what will bring about this sad state of affairs is not Medea's being removed from her children, but her removal of them, by killing them.

1028. *my inflexible will:* the Nurse had earlier referred to Medea's "self-willed mind" (v. 104), and Jason had accused her of acting "stubbornly" (v. 621). This inflexibility, stubbornness, is one of Medea's distinguishing features.

1033. *that you would keep me in old age:* the ancient Greeks thought it a primary duty of children to support their aged parents.

1038. *you will never see Your mother…*1040. *Why do you turn your eyes?…*1043. *see the bright eyes:* see vv. 101 and 860, with notes. The ancients thought that there was something special and uncanny about vision, and in poetry the eyes are often spoken of as a person's quintessential identifying mark.

Women, when I see the bright eyes of the children.
I can not. Good-bye to those plans made
Before. I shall take my children from the land.   1045
Why should I harm them, to hurt their father,
When I would harm myself twice as much?
No, I will not. Farewell to my plans.
And yet, what's wrong? Do I want to be laughed at°
For letting my enemies off scot-free?   1050
The deed *must* be done! How cowardly of me
Even to let soft thoughts° into my mind.
Go into the house, children *(they leave)*. The one for whom
It is not right to attend the sacrifice,°
Beware! But I shall not spoil my work!   1055
Ah! Ah! Do not, my spirit,° do not do this deed!
Let them live—O wretched! Spare the children!
Alive there with us they will gladden you.
No, by those Avenging Demons° in Hades
It is impossible that this should happen, to leave   1060
My children to my enemies to mistreat.   1061
The thing is completely fixed; there is no escape.   1064
Already the crown on her head, wrapped in the robe,   1065
The princess-bride dies. I know it for certain.°
But now I am setting out on a painful road,

1049. *Do I want to be laughed at…?:* we have already heard Medea dreading the prospect of her enemies gloating over her reverses; see vv. 383, 404 and 767.

1052. *soft thoughts:* such signs of weakness are repugnant to Medea, although she was prepared to make a pretense of "soft words" (v. 776) when it was expedient to do so.

1053ff. *The one for whom…attend the sacrifice:* Medea uses the formal language of one preparing a solemn sacrifice, with a warning to outsiders or non-adherents to the cult to depart. Here, the "sacrifice" is the slaying of her children.

1056ff. *Do not, my spirit…:* in the best poetic tradition going back at least to Archilochus in the seventh century, Medea addresses her *thumos*, "spirit," "inner self"—in some contexts, even, "self-consciousness"—as if it were an independent force driving an individual to act in a certain way. And in Medea's case this explanation is perhaps near the truth. (Diggle follows Bergk and Reeve in deleting the whole passage 1056-80; this seems to me unnecessary).

1059. *Avenging Demons:* these were thought of as supernatural agents called up by victims of aggression to seek vengeance on their aggressors; sometimes they were identified with the curses of the injured party.

1062-3. Following Pierson and others, I have left these lines out of the translation, since they are repeated at vv. 1240-1 below, where they seem more in place.

1065-6. *Already the crown…I know it for certain:* this seems to be wishful thinking on Medea's part rather than extrasensory vision of the girl's actual death.

And sending them on one more painful still.
I wish to talk to the children.

(She nods to an attendant to fetch them.)

Give, children,°
Give your right hands to your mother to kiss.   1070
O dearest hands, lips dearest to me
And form and face of my children so well born,
Be fortunate—but there; for matters here
Your father has destroyed. O sweet embrace,
O soft skin, most pleasant breath of my children,   1075
Go, go! *(They leave)*. I am no longer able to look
Upon you. I have lost out against the evils.
I understand how evilly I am about to act,
But my spirit is stronger than my will to resist,
Spirit, the greatest cause of evil for men.°   1080

Choral Interlude°

I have often gone°
Through subtle debates, searched
The fine points of argument

1069 ff. *give, children, Give your right hands. etc:* a very moving account of the display of affection between parent and child, with its delineation of every detail of the children's youthful charm. The poet is exploiting to the full the poignancy of this last farewell—and showing us how strong are the maternal instincts which Medea has had to suppress.

1078-80. *I understand...cause of evil for men:* these verses were quoted frequently by ancient moralists and became famous as an expression of the ethical problem of *akrasia*, weakness of will ("I know the right course of action, but don't do it").

1081-115. *Choral Interlude.* The Chorus (or perhaps just the Chorus leader) chant a series of anapaests on the theme, "Children are a lot of trouble and worry, and what good is it anyway if, as often happens, they die young?" It is not clear that Euripides intended to do more than mark the passage of time for Medea's bizarre revenge to work itself out. There is an obvious relevance in that Medea will in fact lose her children after having expended the effort of rearing them (see vv. 1029-31), but the irony (if intentional) seems heavy-handed: vv. 1109-11 imply that the children die unexpectedly from natural causes ("if fate so decrees..."), which hardly applies to Medea's sons.

It is also rather odd to have the Chorus begin on such a personal and conspiratorial note, and with such high-flown language, when really all they mean in their opening verses is that they'd thought about the matter a long time and heard people discussing it. But the "wisdom" which "their Muse has shared" with them is quite commonplace: childlessness, from a certain point of view, may not be such a misfortune as is often thought.

1081. *I have often gone...:* they mean simply that they have given the matter some thought and listened to others' varying views about it (see end of preceding note).

More than befits a woman.°
But we, too, have a Muse° 1085
Who shares her wisdom with us—
Not with all, but a small
Segment° of women might be found
To be not uncultured.
My conclusion is° that people 1090
Who've never borne children
Are much happier
Than parents.
The childless have no experience
Whether children bring happiness 1095
Or sorrow—They don't have them!
They've missed many sufferings.
But those who have at home
A delightful brood, I see them
Worn out by constant concerns: 1100
First, how to feed and raise them,
And leave them enough to live on.
Then, whether they're laboring
For good children or bad
Is unclear. 1105
I'll mention one last evil,
The worst of all for humans:
Let's say they've successfully raised them;
Their children are now grown up,
And they're good; then, if Fate
So decrees, Death snatches 1110
The children away to Hades.
What profit, then,
If the gods add to woes
This most painful grief,
Only for the sake of children? 1115

1084. *More than befits a woman:* because women, in ancient Greece, were supposed to be seen—sometimes—but almost never heard; in other words, they were expected to maintain submissiveness and dependency on the males about them.

1085. *we, too, have a Muse:* elevated (perhaps unjustifiably so) language; they mean, women are not brainless, as is often supposed. (The tone is similar to that of the first part of the First Choral Ode, vv. 410 ff, although the content is substantially different.)

1087. *Not with all, but a small Segment…:* there is some sarcasm here, but it is not clear how strongly intended it is, nor what its exact point is.

1090. *My conclusion is…..:* after the elaborate build-up, the sequel seems rather banal.

Medea

> My friends, I've waited and watched a long time,
> To learn how things turned out over there.

> *(A Messenger enters from stage-left. He is extremely agitated.)*

> Now finally I see this man coming,
> One of Jason's attendants. His troubled breathing
> Shows that he has some bad news to report.   1120

Messenger

> Woman, you've done a terrible, criminal, thing.°
> Medea, run, run away! Take any
> Conveyance, a ship or chariot, that you can.

Medea

> What happened, then, to warrant such hasty flight?

Messenger

> Died, they've just now died. The princess   1125
> And Creon her father, died because of your poisons.

Medea

> The best possible word° you could speak! You'll be
> For ever after among my benefactors and friends!

Messenger

> What are you saying? Are you sane, not mad, woman,
> Who committed outrage against the royal hearth   1130
> And show delight, not fear, in hearing the news?

Medea

> I, too, am able to give an account
> To match yours.° But take your time, my friend;
> Tell me, then, how did they die? For twice
> The pleasure you'll give,° if they died a horrible death.   1135

1121. Diggle follows some manuscripts in omitting this line. I prefer to retain it.

1127. *The best possible word:* she is referring to the first word of the Messenger's previous statement, "died." This almost ghoulish glee that Medea takes in savoring every grisly detail of her victims' death-agonies shocks and horrifies the Messenger, and us. He cannot believe that she is not insane (v. 1129).

1132-3. *an account To match yours:* her meaning is not entirely clear. Presumably she means she could justify her actions by going over yet again the tale of her mistreatment by Jason and his new in-laws.

1134-5. *For twice The pleasure you'll give:* a particularly macabre (and modern-sounding) touch.

Messenger°

When the two children whom you bore went
With their father and came into the bridal quarters,
We servants who were suffering with your troubles
Were gladdened to hear the rumor going around
That you and your husband had settled your previous quarrel.　　　　1140
One of us kissed a child's hand, another
A golden head. But I, because of my joy,
Followed the children into the women's quarters.
The mistress whom we now respect in your place,
Before she saw your two children come in,　　　　1145
Kept her gaze eagerly fixed on Jason.°
But then she held her veil before her eyes
And turned her white cheek in the other direction,
Out of loathing at the children's entry. Your husband
Tried to dispel the girl's livid anger　　　　1150
By saying to her: "Please don't be angry at dear ones;
Put aside your wrath and turn your head;
Please consider my loved ones yours as well.
Take the gifts and, as a favor to me,
Ask your father° to save these children from exile."　　　　1155
The girl, when she saw the finery, couldn't resist,
But agreed to all her husband's requests, and he
And your sons had not proceeded far from the palace,
When she took and put on the embroidered dress
And placed the golden tiara upon her locks,　　　　1160
Arranging her hair in a brightly reflecting mirror,
And smiling at her body's lifeless image° she saw.
Then she got up from her chair and walked around
The house, skipping lightly with delicate feet,
Thoroughly pleased with the gifts, again and again　　　　1165
Looking behind to make sure the hem was straight.
　　What happened from here on was a terrible sight:
Her fair skin began to change; she stumbled

1136-1230. The Messenger follows Medea's instructions to "take his time," for his account fills almost one hundred lines. For grim realism and horrible detail, it is matched only by the Messenger's account of the killing of Pentheus in *Bacchae* (see, there, vv. 1043 ff., especially 1114-52).

1146. *Kept her gaze eagerly fixed on Jason:* it appears, then, that if for Jason the marriage was a calculated act of self-interest, for his bride it was a love-match.

1155. *Ask your father:* he is thus following Medea's instructions (vv. 942-3).

1162. *her body's lifeless image:* ironical, in view of what will soon befall.

Sideways; her body shook. She hardly managed
To reach her chair without falling flat on the floor.   1170
One of her old serving women, supposing
That a fit of Pan° or some other god was upon her,
Shouted out; then saw around her mouth
The white foam oozing, the eyes in their sockets
Rolling wildly, the color all gone from her skin.   1175
Then, in place of her earlier cry, she let out
A long wail. At once a maid rushed
To her father's quarters, another to tell the new
Husband of his bride's misfortune; the whole house
Resounded with pounding of running peoples' feet.   1180
Before a swift runner could have run
His course and come back to the starting-point,
The girl came out of her faint, opened her eyes
And let out a terrible moan in her misery.
For a double agony was now assaulting her: 1185
First the gold diadem which lay upon her head
Sent out a remarkable stream of devouring flame,
And also her fine-wrought robe, your children's gift,
Was tearing the white skin of the unfortunate girl.
She got up from her chair and ran, all on fire,   1190
Shaking her hair and her head this way, that way,
Trying to cast off the crown. But fixed fast
The gold binding held, and the fire, as she shook
Her hair, simply flared up twice as strong.
She fell to the floor, overmastered by her misfortune,   1195
Unrecognizable to anyone but a parent;°
The usual look of her eyes could not be seen,
Nor her lovely face, but down from the top of her head
Was dripping blood all mixed together with fire.
And from her bones the flesh oozed like resin°   1200
Rent by the poison's hidden jaws; it was
A dreadful sight. For all of us were afraid
To touch the corpse; what happened to her was a lesson.

1172. *a fit of Pan:* such occurrences, especially sudden and violent reactions in an individual or group, were attributed to Pan (hence the word "panic").

1196. *Unrecognizable to anyone but a parent:* a pathetic touch, which also prepares the way for her father's entry and emotional reaction.

1197–1200. *down from the top of her head…blood all mixed together with fire…flesh oozed like resin:* vivid, but perhaps overstepping the bounds of good taste and with more than a touch of "Grand Guignol" (theater of horror).

Her father, poor wretch,° unaware of the disaster,
Burst into the house and fell upon the corpse.   1205
At once he groaned and threw his arms around her,
Kissed her and spoke as follows: "My unlucky child,
Which divinity destroyed you so shamefully?
Which one deprives my aged tomb° of you?
O God, I wish I could die with you,° child!"   1210
When he had brought his sobs and laments to an end
And tried to make his aged body rise
He stuck fast to her woven garments like ivy
To branches of bay,° and there was terrible wrestling:
He wanted to get up on his knees and rise,   1215
But she held fast. If he used force and pulled,
He tore the aged flesh from his bones in shreds.°
Finally the ill-starred man gave up the ghost
And expired; the suffering was too much for him.
They lie now, corpses, child and aged father   1220
Together, a calamity that calls for tears.
    No account need be taken of your situation,
For you will devise an escape from punishment.
I have often considered the human condition a shadow,°
And I would not hesitate to say that those   1225
Who seem to be wise and concern themselves with learning,
These risk being called the biggest fools.
For no mortal man is truly blessed;
When wealth flows one may have more luck
Than another, but is not for that reason blessed.   1230

1204 ff. *Her father, poor wretch:* in a sense the scene has been building to this encounter between loving father and doomed daughter; one aspect of the "children theme" thus reaches its grim conclusion.

1209. *my aged tomb:* a bold metaphor, and touched with irony (for he soon will be as dead as a tomb).

1210. *I wish I could die with you:* again, the phrase is laced with irony.

1213-14. *like ivy To branches of bay:* the image, for all its poignancy, seems overdone.

1216-17. *If he used force…from his bones in shreds:* see my note on vv. 1197-1200. (The Greek word translated "tore…in shreds" is regularly used to describe the rending of an animal victim in the frenzied rites of Dionysus.)

1221. This verse, deleted by Diggle, following Reeve, seems to me unobjectionable.

1224. *the human condition a shadow:* a very frequent image in Greek poetry to describe the transitoriness of human happiness and its susceptibility to reversals.

The sententiousness of these concluding lines by the Messenger (to 1230) may be offensive to modern tastes, but they are a quite conventional aspect of this type of speech; and for all their being truisms, they are true, and timelessly so. (*Bacchae* vv. 1150-2 is a similar close.)

Chorus

  It seems that fate has inflicted on Jason today
  A mass of sufferings, but with justification.
  Poor girl, Creon's daughter, how you stir
  Our pity, who have gone to Hades' halls
  In death,° on account of your marriage-bond with Jason.   1235

Medea

  My friends, I have decided to kill the children
  Without delay and quickly depart from this country;
  I shall not, by delaying, give my children over
  To another,° more unfriendly, hand to murder.
  In any case, their death is inevitable, and since   1240
  It is, I who gave them birth shall kill them.
  Up then! Arm yourself, my heart! Why wait
  To do the dreadful evil that must be done?
  Come, my wretched hand, take up the sword,
  Take it and go to life's goal of grief,°   1245
  Do not be cowardly, do not remember the children,
  How dear they are, how you bore them; for this short day
  At least forget all about your children,
  Then grieve. For even if you kill them, still,
  You bore them, you loved them. I am an unlucky woman.°   1250

Fifth Choral Ode°

  Earth and dazzling   A

1234-5. *have gone to Hades' halls In death:* a standard image applied to (among other Greek heroines) Antigone (Diggle in fact follows Weil in deleting vv. 1233-5).

1238-9. *I shall not…give my children over To another:* in a sense, Medea's hand has been forced by her having employed them to kill the princess. For the version of the story in which her children actually were slain by the people of Corinth, in retribution for the murder of their royal family, see Introduction.

1245. *life's goal of grief:* an athletic metaphor.

1246-50. *do not remember the children…I am an unlucky, etc:* we are left with an impression of Medea the mother, whose instincts of nurture and protection of her young, though suppressed and perhaps perverted, nevertheless still run deep within her. The messenger at v. 1229 had made the point of what an ephemeral thing "good luck" is; for Medea it has entirely passed, and what awaits her is a life of misery (v. 1245).

Fifth Choral Ode (1251-1292) As often the Chorus sing a song to "cover" the decisive action occurring offstage. Stanzas A and A¹, pitched at a high emotional level as they are, contain (besides textual uncertainties) phrases whose meaning is ambiguous, but the over-all sense is clear: since the Sun's divine blood flows in Medea's veins (see, e.g., v. 406), murdering her children is sacrilegious. What is the point of having borne children, if you later kill them? Such a great crime calls for divine vengeance. The third stanza (B) is interrupted by dialogue from the boys within, as they are being murdered (this seems a particularly grisly touch). In

Ray of Sun,° look down, look down
On this murderous woman.
Keep her from laying a bloody hand
On her own children.
From your golden race   1255
She sprang; we are afraid that a god's blood may flow
Because of men's misdeeds.
Stop her, prevent it, O God-given light;
Drive from the house the wretched, murderous Fury of Vengeance°   1260
Empty your labor°   A¹
Of childbirth, empty now and gone;
Lost the lovely
Offspring you bore when you left the straits
Unwelcoming, the dark
And clashing rocks.°
Poor woman! Why does your heart's bile flow   1265
Resulting in violent death?
Grievous the pollution of kin-blood spilt;
It stirs up answering woes from heaven to assault their house.°   1270

Boy (within)

Ah!   1270a

Chorus

Do you hear, do you hear, the children's cry?   B   1273
O miserable unfortunate woman!   1274

---

stanza B¹ the Chorus scour the traditional tales for an analogue to such a horrendous crime,
and can only come up with one, the case of Ino.

1251-2. *Earth...Ray of Sun:* two powerful primal elements (personified), to whom characters
   often appeal in tense situations, even in preference to the Olympian gods. An appeal to the
   Sun is additionally appropriate, since Medea is his grand-daughter.

1260. *Fury of Vengeance:* Medea seems to be identified with the Erinys, or Fury, an earth goddess
   who with her sisters avenged crimes against family members or others of dependent status.
   ("of Vengeance": the text here is uncertain, but there seems to be a reference to the *Alastor*,
   or "avenging demon"; see note on v. 1059.)

1261. *Empty your labor, etc.:* they echo a sentiment expressed earlier by Medea herself (see vv.
   1029 ff.).

1263-4. *The straits unwelcoming...And clashing rocks:* see v. 2 above, with note.

1268-70. The meaning of the Greek text here is exceedingly unclear, but the main ideas seem
   to be as I have given them in the translation.

1270 ff. I give Diggle's line-ordering, and numeration.

Boy

    —O, what should I do? Where run from mother's attack?   1271

    —*(another voice)* I don't know, dearest brother. We're slain!   1272

Chorus

    Should I go into the house? I think I should try   1275

    To save the children from death.

Boy

    Yes, by the gods, save us. We are in need.

    (other) For now the netted sword° is near us, strikes.

Chorus

    Wretched woman, you must have been rock°

    Or iron to kill the children seedlings you bore   1280

    With a doom which you inflicted.

    Of one woman, one only I have heard   B¹

    That she cast her hand at her own dear children:

    Ino,° maddened by God, when Zeus' wife

    Expelled her° from home to wander.   1285

    She impiously killed her children and leapt,

    Poor wretch, into the sea,

    Stepping over an ocean cliff,

    Dying with the two children she slew.

    What, I ask, could be more terrible?   1290

    O, the suffering that women's love-life brings!

    The harm done among humans!°

1278. *the netted sword:* probably not literal, but a metaphor: "we are caught in a trap (consisting in) the sword." Note the convention that killing was not actually depicted on the Greek stage here comes close to being broken, since the boys' vivid account and blood-curdling shrieks make us feel we are actually present at the murder.

1279-80. *You must have been rock....* the point is made yet again that Medea is something inhuman, an elemental force of nature (see v. 29 and elsewhere).

1284. *Ino:* Ino, about whom Euripides also wrote a tragedy, was a daughter of Cadmus of Thebes and the typical "evil stepmother" to her husband Athamas' children by his first marriage. In punishment the goddess Hera drove her mad and, after killing one of her sons by Athamas, she leapt with the other into the sea. (There were other examples of mythical mothers who slew their children—e.g. Procne and Agave—but these are conveniently ignored so the Chorus can make the point that there was "one woman, one only" who had acted as terribly as Medea.)

1284-5. *Zeus' wife Expelled her:* Hera, who had befriended Athamas' children; the implication is that, as noted above, she drove Ino insane.

1291-2. The Chorus ends its song by drawing a general conclusion, not only from Ino's case but also Medea's (compare Jason's oversimplification, vv. 569 ff.).

(Jason rushes in.)°

Jason

Women, who stand in attendance near this house,
Is the one who did these terrible things, Medea,
Still at home, or has she made good her escape?   1295
She must now either hide beneath the earth
Or take wing and fly° up to heaven's height
To avoid reprisals from the household of the King.
Is she sure she can kill the princes of the land,
And then escape from this house, free and unpunished?   1300
Still, I care less for her than for the children;°
She will fall victim in turn to those she wronged.
I have come, however, to save my children's lives,
To keep the king's family from making them pay
For the foul murder° committed by their mother.   1305

Chorus Leader

Poor Jason! You do not know what evil
You're in, or else you wouldn't have spoken like that.

Jason

What is it? I suppose she wants to kill me, too.

Chorus Leader

Your children are dead. Their mother's hand killed them.

Jason

Ah! What are you saying? You've destroyed me, woman!°   1310

Chorus Leader

Realize finally that your children are no more.

Jason

Where did she kill them? Inside or outside the house?

(Jason rushes in.) It is noteworthy that in this final scene Jason is portrayed as far more believably human, even sympathetic, than he has been up until now. Suffering seems to have ennobled him, or at least to have made him less pompous.

1297. *take wing and fly:* Jason has no idea how close he is to describing the way in which Medea actually will escape.

1301. *I care less for her than for the children:* he does *not* come in saying "what she did to my bride!"; we are about to discover how much Jason really cares for his sons.

1304-5. *making them pay For the foul murder:* such possible reprisals had been envisaged by Medea (vv. 1238-9).

1310. *You've destroyed me, woman!:* he addresses Medea, although he cannot see her.

Chorus Leader

If you open the doors you will see your children's bodies.

Jason

(shouts) Attendants, unlock the bolts as fast as you can,
Release the latches; let me see the double   1315
Evil, the victims, their killer whom I'll punish.
(Medea appears on the roof in a chariot.)°

Medea

Why are you trying to move and unbar the gates,
Seeking the corpses and me who made them so?
Stop your exertions. If you need something from me,
Tell me what you want; you shall never touch me.   1320
This chariot here my father's father, the Sun-god,°
Has given to me, to ward off my enemies' might.

Jason

You hateful creature! Woman by far most loathsome,
To gods, to me, and to the entire human race,
A mother, you had the nerve to thrust a sword   1325
Into your children, thus making me a childless
Ruin; and doing this, you look upon
The sun and earth,° though daring the foulest of crimes?
Go to damnation! My sense has returned, though then
I lacked it when I took you from home and a foreign land   1330
And brought you to a Greek home, a great evil,
Betrayer of your father° and the land that gave you birth.
The gods have inflicted your Avenger° against me.

1317. Medea's appearance "above," on the roof of the stage-building or suspended from the so-called "machine," comes as a shock, to the audience as well as to Jason. Although from her remarks to Aigeus earlier that she would "come to his city by the quickest means" (v. 757) we might have supposed that she was thinking about a way of escaping from Corinth, nothing has suggested this particular supernatural conveyence. It takes the place of the device with which many of Euripides' other plays end, the "god or goddess (speaking) from the machine."

1321. *my father's father, the Sun-god:* her descent from the Sun had been referred to repeatedly earlier in the play (cf. vv. 406, 476-7, 954-5).

1327-8. *You look upon The Sun and earth:* Medea as it were desecrates the purity of these elemental forces, the same ones as the Chorus had called upon at vv. 1251-2.

1332. *Betrayer of your father:* he repeats the accusation which she had so often made against herself (vv. 31-2, 166-7, 502-3, 799 ff.; and cf. vv. 441 ff., 643 ff.).

1333. *your Avenger:* for this "avenging Spirit" see note on v. 1059. Jason seems to mean that he is now being punished for his complicity in Medea's previous crimes (so Flacelière).

After killing the brother who shared your hearth,° you went
Aboard the Argo, the ship of beautiful prow,   1335
Such were the beginnings you started from. You married
This husband then and bore children to me,
But because of the bed and sex you murdered them.
No Greek woman would ever have dared
This. Yet I ranked you over them, and married   1340
You, a wife who hated and ruined me,
A lioness not a woman,° who have a nature
More fierce even than that of Etruscan Scylla.°
But not by casting ten thousand insulting remarks
Could I injure you, so brash is your inborn nature.   1345
Be damned, shamefully defiled with your children's blood!
It is left for me now to lament my fate.
Now I shall never enjoy my new bride's bed,
Nor be able to speak to the children I bred and raised
Yet alive in this world, for I have lost them.   1350

Medea

I would have made a long speech refuting
Your arguments, if father Zeus didn't know
What you got from me and what you did in return.
You were not about to treat my bed with dishonor
And spend a pleasant life laughing at me.°   1355
Nor were the princess and her father who gave her to you
Going to exile me and get off scot-free.
So call me, if you like, a lioness,
A Scylla° who dwells in the land of Etruria,
For I've fittingly driven my sting into your heart.   1360

1334. *who shared your hearth:* another interpretation of this phrase is "at the hearth" (the ancient marginal commentator says it means "in the palace").

1342. *A lioness not a woman:* the Nurse had earlier said that Medea's glare was like that of a "mother lioness" (v. 188). The theme of Medea's bestial nature is thus rounded off (see vv. 29, 92 with note, 103, 1279-80).

1343. *Estruscan Scylla:* the monster described by Homer (*Odyssey* 12.89 ff.; cf. Vergil, *Aeneid* 3.420 ff.) as having six heads with three rows of teeth, and twelve feet, which snatched sailors as they sailed through the straits of Messene between Sicily and Italy in the direction of that part of the Mediterranean called by the Greeks the "Tyrrhenian," or Etruscan, Sea.

1355. *laughing at me:* for the theme of the intolerability of having enemies gloat over one's setbacks see vv. 383, 404, 797 and 1049.

1359. *Scylla:* see note on v. 1343 (Diggle, following Verrall, condemns this line, since "land of Etruria" seems an odd expression; some have emended to "cave" or "strait").

Jason

Yet you grieve, too, and share in the disaster.

Medea

True, but grief is gain, if it stops you from laughing.

Jason

O children, what an evil mother you encountered!

Medea

O children, how your father's illness° killed you!

Jason

At least it wasn't my right hand that killed them.   1365

Medea

No, your insults and your recent marriage.

Jason

Was it really for sex that you decided to kill them?

Medea

Do you think that this is small suffering° for a woman?

Jason

A self-controlled one,° but for you a world of evil.

Medea

These children no longer live; *that* will wound you.   1370

Jason

They live on, alas!, as Avenging Spirits° for *you*.

Medea

The gods know who began to inflict suffering.

Jason

And they know, truly, how loathsome your heart is.

1364. *your father's illness:* a slightly unusual way of referring to Jason's behavior in abandoning her for the princess. (Perhaps she is imputing madness to him.)

1368. *Do you think that this is a small suffering...?:* Medea seems to confirm the charge made by Jason at vv. 569 ff., and which the Chorus echoed at vv. 1291-2.

1369. *A self-controlled one:* "self-control" was the virture by which Jason had set so much stock (see vv. 549, 635, 884, with notes and cf. 913).

1371. *Avenging Spirits:* he means that the children's deaths will "cry to heaven for vengeance" and that (he hopes) Medea will be punished for her crime by some divine agency.

Medea

Loathe on, then. I detest your shrill barking.

Jason

And I yours. We are easily done with each other.   1375

Medea

How? What should I do? I very much want to.

Jason

Give me the corpses to bury and then grieve for.

Medea

No, indeed, my hand will bury them,
After bringing them to Hera's shrine on the cliff,°
So none of my enemies will insult them by pulling   1380
Down their tombs. In this country of Sisyphus,°
We shall assign a sacred feast and rituals°
As a future memorial of this impious crime.
I myself am going to Erechtheus' country,°
Athens, to live with Aigeus, son of Pandion.   1385
Since you are base, your death will be fittingly mean:
You'll be struck on the head by a piece of your ship, Argo,°
A bitter termination to your marriage with me.

1379. *Hera's shrine on the cliff:* an important sanctuary of Hera, who had "on the cliff" as one of her cult-titles at Corinth and elsewhere; the ancient sources are not very clear about its location (perhaps in the direction of Sicyon on the Gulf of Lechaion).

1381. *country of Sisyphus:* Corinth, see note on v. 405.

1382. *We shall assign a sacred feast and rituals:* several of Euripides' plays end with a similar charter for the performance of some such generally quite minor local festival, and many of these are known from the sources to have been celebrated until much later than the poet's own time (for this one, see Pausanias 2.3.6). It is not clear what the poet's purpose was in thus connecting an occurrence in his play with an actual contemporary event. (Note that a memorial celebrated by the people of Corinth in honor of Medea's sons makes more sense with the version of the story that had the children murdered by the people, who later tried to expiate their deed by setting up a festival.)

1384. *Erechtheus' country:* see note on v. 824.

1387. *Struck on the head by a piece of your ship, Argo:* a similar (although not identical) version is credited to Staphylus; see Plot Summaries (a)(i). There were other variants: Jason had dedicated the mast of the Argo in Hera's temple, but as he was going out it fell on him and killed him (ancient note on *Medea* 1286); or Medea predicted that Jason would commit suicide (Neophron).

Jason

May the children's avenging Fury° and Justice°
For murder destroy you!   1390

Medea

What god, what spirit, listens to you,
Breaker of oaths,° deceiver of friends?

Jason

You polluted slayer of your children!°

Medea

Go home and bury your bride!

Jason

I am going, deprived of my two children.   1395

Medea

There's more lamenting to come—wait for old age.°

Jason

O dearest children!

Medea

Dearest to their mother, not to you.

Jason

And yet you killed?

Medea

To cause you pain.°

Jason

O, I am miserable. I wish I could
Kiss the dear lips of my children.   1400

1389-end. This closing section of the play between Medea and Jason is in anapaests, a rhythm which denotes a rise in the level of excitement.

1389. *the children's avenging Fury:* see v. 1371 and note on v. 1260. Furies were often said to work as agents or emissaries of the personified goddess Justice (Medea had herself invoked Justice at v. 764.)

1392. *breaker of oaths:* a final time Medea returns to her charge of faithlessness against Jason (see v. 162-3, 209-10, 439, 492, 495).

1393. *polluted slayer of your children:* the level of invective rises.

1396. *Wait for old age:* she means that if he somehow survives the falling ship-timber (v. 1387) and lives to old age, he will have no offspring to perform the expected tendance on elderly parents (for this solemn duty, see note on v. 1033).

1398. *To cause you pain:* Medea puts her motive with razor-like simplicity.

Medea

Now talk to, embrace, them!
Before, you drove them away.

Jason

In God's name
Allow me to touch° the soft skin of the children.

Medea

It cannot be. Your words have been uttered in vain.

Jason

Zeus, do you hear how I am rejected?   1405
Do you see what she is doing to me,
This polluted child-murdering lioness?°
But with the breath and force that are in me
I will raise a dirge, and summon the gods,
Calling on them to witness° how you   1410
Killed my children and now keep me
From touching and burying their bodies,
Whom I wish I had never begotten
To see them murdered by you. *(Medea disappears)*.

Chorus

Zeus, Olympus' steward, controls many things,°   1415
And many things, too, beyond expectation the gods accomplish.
The expected does not turn out;
For the unexpected God finds a way.
Such is the end of this business.

1402. *In God's name allow me to touch:* Jason's moving appeal does not move Medea. We sympathize with the anguished father in a way that would have seemed impossible because of the highly unfavorable impression he made in the earlier scenes.

1407. *polluted child-mudering lioness:* he repeats some of the language of v. 1393 and the animal image of v. 1342.

1409-10. *summon the gods, Calling on them to witness:* this reminds us of an earlier legalism by Jason (v. 619), but he has far more justification here.

1415-19. Some critics (including Diggle) excise these final anapaestic lines by the Chorus on the grounds that they are bland and are found in almost the same form at the end of *Andromache, Helen, Bacchae* and *Alcestis*. But they seem inoffensive°enough and by their very conventionality would have served notice to the audience that the play really was over.

Appendices

(a)(i) Plot Summaries[1]

After coming to Corinth and bringing Medea with him, Jason marries as well Glauke, daughter of Creon, King of Corinth. When Medea is about to be exiled from Corinth by Creon, she asks to remain one additional day and obtains this request; she sends gifts to Glauke through her children as repayment for this favor, a dress and a gold crown, but when Glauke puts them on she perishes, and when Creon embraces his daughter, he dies as well. After killing her own children, Medea becomes a passenger in a chariot drawn by winged dragons, which she received from the Sun-god, and she escapes to Athens; there, she weds Aigeus, king of Athens. Pherecydes and Simonides[2] report that Medea made Jason young by cooking him. The poet of *The Returns*[3] writes as follows about Jason's father Aison:

> Immediately she made Aison a dear lad in the bloom of youth, after she had stripped away his old age with her cunning wits by cooking many drugs in golden cauldrons.

Aeschylus in his play *Nurses of Dionysus*[4] tells that she also rejuvenated Dionysus' nurses by cooking them along with their husbands. Staphylus[5] says that Jason was killed by Medea in some such way: she told him to go to sleep beneath the stern of

---

1. Some ancient manuscripts contain part or all of these "plot summaries"(designated *Hypothesis* by ancient scholars). The material goes back to the great age of Alexandrian scholarship (third to first centuries B.C.), and much of the factual information derives from official records.

2. Pherecydes was an Athenian prose-writer, working in the first part of the fifth century B.C., who wrote genealogies of leading families and recounted many of the major myths. Euripides seems to have drawn on him in several places in his plays. Simonides was a celebrated poet who worked at Samos, Athens, Thessaly and elsewhere between about 525 and 470 B.C. He is also reported as having mentioned Jason's joint-rule with Medea at Corinth.

3. "The Returns" was one of several poems composed to complete Homer's version of the Trojan saga (these are sometimes referred to as "cyclic epics"). Some sources names its author as a certain Hagias of Trozen, of unknown date.

4. Beyond the information given here, nothing is known about this lost drama of Aeschylus, which may have been a satyr-play, and so would have had comic elements.

5. Staphylus of Naucratis was an Alexandrian scholar whose dates are unknown (before c. 150 B.C.); he wrote a treatise in at least three books "On the Thessalians," and several other ethnographic works.

the "Argo" (the ship being on the verge of disintegrating from age); when the stern in fact fell on Jason, he died.[6]

Euripides appears to have taken over the arrangements of the drama from Neophron,[7] as Dicaearchus[8] says in [Book 1] of his *Life of Greece* and Aristotle in the *Commentaries*. They criticize him (i.e. Euripides) for not having Medea maintain her character but resorting to tears when she was laying her plot against Jason and his wife. But the opening is praised for its extravagantly emotional quality, and of the elaboration of the theme "in the forest glens…" (v.3), and what follows. In ignorance of this Timachidas[9] says that Euripides dealt first with an event that came later, as Homer does:

> (Calypso) after having put fragrant garments on him and bathed him (*Odyssey* 5.264)

(ii) Summary by Aristophanes the literary scholar[10]

Because of her hatred of Jason for having married Creon's daughter Glauce, Medea killed her, Creon and her own children; then she left Jason to cohabit with Aigeus. This plot was not used by either Aeschylus or Sophocles. The drama is set in Corinth, and the Chorus consists of women of the city. Medea's nurse delivers the prologue. It was performed in Pythodorus' archonship, the first year of the 87th Olympiad (i.e., spring 431 B.C.). Euphorion[11] was first, Sophocles second, and Euripides third with *Medea*, *Philoctetes*, *Dictys* and the satyr-drama *Harvesters* which is lost.

Characters in the drama: Nurse, Tutor, Medea, Chorus of Women, Creon, Jason, Aigeus, Messenger, Medea's sons.

---

6. See v. 1387 with note.

7. See Introduction pp. 5-6 for Euripides' alleged "borrowings" from Neophron.

8. Dicaearchus of Messene was a pupil of Aristotle and one of the so-called "Peripatetics"; he interested himself in literary scholarship. The works mentioned here do not survive, and some scholars in fact deny that the *Commentaries* were by Aristotle.

9. Timachidas of Rhodes was one of the authors of the Lindian Temple chronicle (first century B.C.) which survives on stone. What he seems to object to is that Euripides reverses the chronological order of events: the Argo is already on her way (vv. 1 ff.), and then Euripides mentions the construction (vv. 3-4).

10. Aristophanes of Byzantium (c. 200 B.C.) was a literary scholar and head librarian at Alexandria, who produced editions of the major Greek "classic" authors, including the dramatists. The Plot Summary that follows is probably not by him.

11. Euphorion was a son of Aeschylus and a dramatist himself, who was said to have won several victories with his father's previously unproduced plays.

(b) ... 2nd, *Medea,* which begins[12]

"I wish that the ship Argo had never flown..." The plot:
...the murder of Pelias
after he had become (? a fugitive) (Jason) came to Corinth... (having brought
Medea there)
and made a request...of Creon
The King... Medea
(revealing) her barbaric character and (savage)
spirit wanted to take (vengeance) Creon ordered her
to go into exile along with the children...
but when she asked him (to let her stay just one day) he
agreed. She thereupon ... (and)
got the advantage. For the chance arrival
of Aigeus... (she persuaded him)
to receive her (at Athens)...
When she replied... (she sent the children)
bearing gifts to Glauke a gold-
en crown, because of which...
(She) painfully left (? life)...
tore away (her flesh). Her father (rushing)
to assist his daughter... (was unable)
to draw away from her...

---

12. From a papyrus of the second century A.D. (Pap. IFAO [Cairo], PSP 248). Words in brackets are supplements.

Suggestions For Further Reading

Articles

Barlow, Shirly A. "Stereotype and reversal in Euripides' *Medea*," *Greece & Rome* 2 ser. 36 (1989) 158-171. "In the end [Medea] allows her very strong love as a mother, essential to her feminine nature, to be trampled by a heroic resolve which a man would normally direct towards military enemies, colleagues in arms, or at least opponents who are not of kindred blood, but which she, in her extremity, turns upon these innocent objects [her children] who are her own flesh and blood" (p. 169).

Bongie, Elizabeth B. "Heroic elements in the *Medea* of Euripides," *Transactions of the American Philological Association (TAPA)* 107 (1977) 27-56. "It is Medea's consistent and unwavering dedication to the principles of the heroic code that, more than any other single factor, binds Euripides' great tragedy into a coherent whole" (p. 56).

Browne, R.A. "*Medea*: interpretations," in M. E. White, ed., *Studies in honor of Gilbert Norwood* (Toronto, 1952) 76-79. "...I have begun to wonder whether [Aigeus] has not come specifically to consult [Medea]" (p. 77). "The sensational effects of the magic preparations [described by the Messenger at vv. 1136-1221] come out all the more powerfully because so little was said to prepare the audience for the blood-curdling sequel" (p. 78).

Burnett, A. P. "Medea and the tragedy of revenge," *Classical Philology (CP)* 68 (1973) 1-24. "Petty and flawed and corrupt as [Jason] is, he is properly destroyed by a secular female enemy who represents in herself not so much the religion of the proud Olympians as the very magic of the older gods that Jason thought to use and cast away" (p. 17).

Buttery, T.V. "Accident and design in Euripides' *Medea*," *American Journal of Philology (AJP)* 79 (1958) 1-17. "The third episode [the Aigeus scene, vv. 663-823] occupies the exact center of the tragedy, serving as a pivot on which both action and emotion turn. The two halves of the play thus defined and neatly balanced are almost two different plays. The first is static (emotion never becomes action), deliberate, and rather satisfying to us in our sympathy with Medea (culminating in the great satisfaction, the appearance of Aegeus as savior). The second is active, violent, and horrifying" (p. 10).

Collinge, N.E. "Medea *ex machina*," *CP* 57 (1962) 170-172. "...the effect [of Medea's appearance in the chariot of the Sun, vv. 1317 ff.] is all the greater because...the means by which Medea will escape from Corinth has been a problem in the background all the while the play has proceeded" (p. 171).

Cunningham, M. P. "Medea *apo mêchanês*," *CP* 49 (1954) 151-160. "...the appearance of Medea in the exodos [vv. 1293 ff.] constitutes a sort of visual metaphor emphasizing the utter evil and callousness of Medea and her loss of human qualities as result of what she has done" (p. 160).

Dihle, A. "Euripides' Medea und inhre Schwestern im europäischen Drama," *Antike und Abendland* 22 (1976) 175-184. "Der ingeniose Plan aber, mit dem sie dieses bewirkt [overcoming her enemies in "heroic" fashion], zerstört durch den dabei notwendigen Mord an den Kindern die Grundlage, auf der allein sie als Frau und Mutter leben kann. Der Racheplan ist Resultat eines an vorgegebenen Verhaltensregeln orientierten Kalküls, nicht aber, wie bei den Nachfolgern des Euripides, Ausfluss einer übermächtigen Leidenschaft" (p. 182).

Dunkle, J. Roger "The Aegeus Episode," *TAPA* 100 (1969) 97-107. "As a microcosm of the whole play, the Aegeus scene with the king's surprising arrival at Corinth out of nowhere and subsequent bargain with Medea mirrors the self-interested opportunism and chaotic irrationality which dominate the play" (p. 107).

Dyson, Michael "Euripides *Medea* 1056-1080," *Greek, Roman & Byzantine Studies* [*GRBS*] 28 (1987) 23-24. "Without it [the disputed passage vv. 1056-80; he excises 1026-3], moving as the first part of the monologue is, we never see Medea unreservedly loving her children, as the action of the play demands if we are to feel her as tragic; with it the final embrace leaves no doubt as to her love and her torment" (p. 34).

Easterling, P.E. "The infanticide in Euripides' *Medea*" *Yale Classical Studies* (YCS) 25 (1977) 177-191. "The tragedy is that [Medea] does stand out above the limited and shabby people around her, does have a sharper moral awareness and far greater distinction and force of personality, yet the audience cannot help but shudder at the ruthlessness of her anger and passion for vengeance" (p. 183).

Flory, Stewart "Medea's right hand: promises and revenge," *TAPA* 108 (1978) 69-74. "The touch of the hand undergoes a gradual but complete transformation from the loving and trusting to the deceitful and hostile hand, and finally to the hand stained with blood" (p. 74).

Foley, Helene P. "Medea's divided self," *Classical Antiquity* 8 (1989) 61-85 "*Medea* exposes male suppression of women in marriage and the tragic results of a male re-fusal to recognize in women the same capacities, feelings and needs they accept for themselves; and it shows the corrupting effects of this mistreatment of a woman of tremendous feeling and intelligence. At the same time Medea's overly literal imitation of an anachronistic masculine role, her dehumanization, and her betrayal of her own sex could be said equally to confirm women's ultimate incapacity for independence and civilized behavior" (pp. 82-3).

Fortenbaugh, William W. "On the antecedents of Aristotle's bipartite psychology," *GRBS* 11 (1970) 233-250. "...the *Medea* as a whole and the famous monologue in particular [vv. 1021-80] are especially useful for illustrating and understand Aristotle's moral psychology, because they distinguish implicitly spirit or emotion from *both* deliberation about means *and* also reasoned reflection about emotional responses" (p. 234).

Friedrich, Rainer "*Medea apolis*: on Euripides' dramatization of the crisis of the polis" in A.H. Sommerstein et. al. ed., *Tragedy, comedy and the polis: papers from the Greek Drama Conference, Nottingham, 18-20 July 1990* (Bari, 1993) 219-39. "For the sake of a purely personal tie based on erotic passion [Medea] has severed all ties that bind ancient man and woman to the ethical universe of the polis and to its natural foundation, the *oikos*. She has virtually exiled herself from the *koinonia politike* and thus made herself *apolis* in the most radical sense of the term..." (p. 226).

Gill, C. "Did Chrysippus understand Medea?" *Phronesis* 28 (1983) 136-149 [The Stoic philosopher] Chrysippus does not take Medea's words [at vv. 1078-80] as involving a complete denial of (rational) intentionality in which Medea does not function as a human being at all. He describes her state as that of disobedience and rejection of reason, that is, a recognition, but deliberate rejection, of what a reasonable human being would do in those circumstances" (p. 141).

Gilula, Dwora "On the oracle given to Aegeus (Eur. *Med.* 679, 681)," *Scripta Classica Israelica* 6 (1981/2) 14-18. "...the absence of a mention of Aegeus' childlessness prior to Euripides' *Medea* combined with the fact that childlessness is a focal theme in the tragedy speak forcibly for crediting Euripides with the creation of the Aegeus oracle" (p. 18).

Golden, Leon "Children in the *Medea*", *Classical Bulletin* 48 (1971) 10-15. "Bitter as the searing conflict is between the two protagonists, the most significant emotional effect of the play does not arise from this conflict, but rather, from the brutal victimization of innocent children" (p. 14).

Knox, Bernard M.W. "The *Medea* of Euripides," YCS 25 (1977) 193-225 [reprinted in Knox, *Word and Action, essays on the ancient theater* (Baltimore, 1979) pp. 295-322]. "Euripides is concerned in this play, not with progress or reform, but (just as in the *Hippolytus* and *Bacchae*) with the eruption in tragic violence of forces in human nature which have been repressed and scorned, which in their long-delayed breakout exact a monstrous revenge. The *Medea* is not about woman's rights; it is about woman's wrongs, those done to her and by her" (p. 211).

Mills, S. P. "The sorrows of Medea", *CP* 75 (1980) 289-296. "The first act of vengeance, the murder of Creon and his daughter with the poisoned robe and crown, casts [Medea] in the folktale role of the fairy or demon who loves a mortal man and who tries to dispose of her rival by the treacherous gift of a magic belt or robe. The second vengeance act, the murder of her own children, gives her rather the character of an Ino or a Procne who slays her son(s) to punish their father's infidelity and then, undergoing a metamorphosis, mourns their loss forever after " (p.296).

Musurillo, Herbert, S.J. "Euripides' *Medea*: a reconsideration," *AJP* 87 (1966) 52-74. "In Medea we see the nature of the violent conflict between the softer (and more feminine) and the vicious, more animal side of her nature. Here [in her decision to kill her children] love and hate are inextricably intertwined. The contradictions within her soul are ruthlessly exposed" (p. 64).

Newton, Rick M. "Ino in Euripides' *Medea*," *AJP* 106 (1985) 496-502. "...there are no genuine mythological examples to mitigate the horror of Medea's actions. For Ino [see v. 1284 with note] offers no parallel. Medea's crime, lacking a precedent, is truly *anêkouston* [unheard of]" (p 502).

———— "Medea's passionate poison," *Syllecta Classica* 1 (1989) 13-20. "...[I]t is the mark of Medea to confound the distinction between friend and foe, to transgress the boundary between right and wrong and, consequently, to instill in the spectator a disturbing degree of agitation, *taragmos*." (p. 13)

Reckford, Kenneth J. "Medea's first exit," *TAPA* 99 (1986) 329-359. "...the tragedy of Medea gains force from a background of contemporary Athenian aspirations, at once personal, social, and intellectual; but at the same time Medea is in our play the touchstone by which these aspirations are tested and fail" (p. 346).

Rickert, GailAnn "Akrasia and Euripides' *Medea*", *Harvard Studies in Classical Philology* 91 (1987) 91-117. "[In vv. 1078-80] Medea, confronted by competing claims, can be understood as acting in accordance with her *thumos* and yet simultaneously recognizing the importance of the claims she does not pursue or at least the harm she does through her action" (p.117).

Schein, Seth L. "Philia in Euripides' *Medea*," in M. Griffith and D.J. Mastronarde, edd., *Cabinet of the Muses. Essays in classical and comparative literature in honor of Thomas G. Rosenmeyer* (Atlanta, 1989) pp. 57-73. "Throughout the play, in her successive encounters with Creon, Aegeus, and Jason, Medea uses her understanding of *philia* [love, friendship], and her ability to exploit it and other traditional institutions and relationships of reciprocity, to achieve her own ends and defeat her enemies" (p. 62).

Schlesinger, Eilhard "On Euripides' *Medea*," in Erich Segal, ed. *Oxford Readings in Greek Tragedy* (Oxford, 1983) 294-310 (slightly abridged from the German, published in *Hermes* 94 [1966] 26-53). This antithesis of the male and female world is also a motif which passes through the whole play, above all in the choral odes.... In Euripides, however [as opposed to Homer's presentation of Hector and Andromache in *Iliad*, Book VI], the male world is completely dehumanized. Jason is the child of a noble family, whose every effort is directed exclusively toward gaining status, and whose idea is to live well and to feel no want (559 f). Opposed to him stands Medea as a woman and as a champion of human values and personal relationships." (p. 307).

Séchan, Louis "La légende de Médée," *Revue des études grecques* 40 (1927) 234-310. [a thorough survey of the myths concerning Medea and their variants]

Seidensticker, Bernd "Euripides, *Medea* 1056-1080, an interpolation?," in *Cabinet of the Muses* [See under Schein, above] pp. 89-102. "The numerous passages that, directly or indirectly, bear witness to Medea's anger, hatred, and jealousy certainly justify the statement of 1079 that her passionate and violent temper—her *thumos*—is stronger than the considerations of her motherly love" (p. 98). [Seidensticker also discusses previous scholars' arguments about the genuineness or otherwise of this passage.]

Shaw, Michael "The female intruder: women in fifth-century drama," *CP* 70 (1975) 255-266 [he analyzes *Medea* at pp. 258-264].

Stanton, G.R. "The end of Medea's monologue: Euripides, *Medea* 1078-80," *Rheinisches Museum* 130 (1987) 97-106. "What Medea says [in these verses]...is: "I realise what evil I am about to do, but drive [*thumos*], which is the cause of the most terrible evils for motals, is master of my plans" (p. 106).

Walsh, George B. "Public and private in three plays of Euripides," *CP* 74 (1979) 294-309 (*Medea* at 294-300). "The murder of the children is not an act of hatred against them, any more than Medea's wish to live means that she looks forward to pleasure in life. Both arise from her personal motives, their purpose defined principally in terms of the judgment they may elicit from society" (p. 298).

Books about Euripides, with section on Medea

Conacher, Desmond J. *Euripidean Drama: Myth, Theme and Structure* (Toronto and London, 1967) [pp. 183-198] "Without this scene [vv. 1019 ff.] what Medea eventually becomes would indeed smack of melodrama. That monstrous figure attains tragic significance only when we see it as the result of a conflict—of a victory, as Medea herself expresses it (1079-80)—of her all-consuming passion for vengeance over her better counsels" (p. 196).

Grube, G.M.A. *The Drama of Euripides* (London, 1941; reprinted) [pp. 147-165] "The tragedy of Medea—of love turning to hatred when betrayed, until the woman's whole soul is dominated by a lust for vengeance that overpowers even maternal love—is one which no modern reader should, in its essentials, find difficult to make his own" (p. 147).

Book on Greek drama, with section on Euripides

Kitto, H.D.F. *Greek tragedy, a literary study* (3rd. ed. London, 1961) "[Medea] is tragic in that her passions are stronger than her reason (...[v.] 1097); she is drawn with such vigor and directness, everything that she says and does springs so immediately from her dominant motive that she is eminently dramatic; nevertheless she is not a tragic heroine as we have hitherto understood the term: she is too extreme, too simple" (p. 194).

Books about Euripides' *Medea*

Clauss, James J., and Sarah Iles Johnston, edd., *Medea: Essays on Medea in Myth, Literature, Philosophy, and Art* (Princeton: Princeton Univ. Press, 1997).

McDermott, Emily A. *Euripides' "Medea": the Incarnation of Disorder* (University Park, Penna. and London, 1989)

Papageorgiou, Vasilis *Euripides' Medea and Cosmetics* (Göteborg, 1986) [a reading of the play in "deconstructionist" terms]

Pucci, Pietro *The Violence of Pity in Euripides' "Medea"* (Ithaca N.Y., 1980)

Survey of work on Euripides

Collard, C. *Euripides* [*Greece & Rome: New Surveys in the Classics* 14] (Oxford, 1981)

Text

Diggle, J. *Euripidis Fabulae, Tomus I* (Oxford, 1984)
Kovacs, David *Euripides, Cyclops, Alcestis, Medea* edited and translated [Loeb Classical Library] (Cambridge MA, 1994)

Text with English commentary

Elliott, Alan *Euripides: Medea* (Oxford, 1969)
Page, D.L. *Euripides, Medea* (Oxford, 1938; reprinted)

Text with French commentary

Flacelière, Robert *Euripide, Médée* (Paris, 1970)

Addenda to Revised Printing

des Bouvrie, Synnøve *Women in Greek tragedy. an anthropological approach* [Symbolae Osloenses fasc. suppl. 27] (Oslo, l990) pp. 214-39, "Euripides' *Medeia*". "At the 'tragic' level Jason is destroyed by the absolute loss of descendants... The force of Medeia's part in the drama is to be found at this level: to create a turbulence of violent emotions... Her actions cause a threat to Jason's *oikos* and result in its final disruption" (p.238).

Brelich, Angelo. "I figli di Medea," *Studi e materiali di storia delle religioni* 30 (1959) 213-54. [examines the tradition surrounding the cultic practices allegedly celebrated at Corinth to commemorate the slaying of Medea's children by Medea herself (as in Euripides) or the Corinthians]

Caiazza, Antonio "Medea: fortuna di un mito, prima parte," *Dioniso* 69 (1989) 9-84; "...seconda parte," ibid. 60 (1990) 82-118. [traces fully and often in some detail various literary, theatrical and musical reworkings of the myth up to the twentieth century]

Dunn, Francis "Euripides and the rites of Hera Akraia," *GRBS* 35 (1994) 103-15 "When [Medea] says she will bury the children in Hera's sanctuary we are reminded that Medea (not the Corinthians) killed the children, deliberately (unlike her counterpart in Eumelus); when she says their bodies will be safe from enemies, we are reminded that Medea (not the Corinthians) committed sacrilege against them; and when she says she will establish rites to atone for their murder, we recall that Medea (unlike the Corinthians) will not suffer for her crime" (p. 1 15).

Gredley, Bernard "The place and time of victory: Euripides' *Medea*," *Bulletin of the Institute of Classical Studies*, Univ. of London 34 (1987) 27-39. "The cumulative effect of the two hundred lines before Medea's appearance is to create the sense of her singularity *and* dominance. Following scenes will strengthen the impression through a variety of techniques designed to confirm her control of the performance area and her superiority over Creon, Jason and Aegeus" (p.30).

Hatzichronoglou, Lena "Euripides' Medea: woman or fiend?," in *Woman's power, Man's game. Essays on classical antiquity in honor of Joy C. King* (Chicago, 1933) 178-93. "The *Medea*... depicts vividly the disaster to which the overemphasis on the Greek, aristocratic, male *nomos* ('custom,' 'tradition,' 'law') at the expense of *physis* ('nature') could lead" (p.190).

Luschnig, C.A.E. "Interiors: imaginary spaces in *Alcestis* and *Medea*," *Mnemosyne* 4 ser. 45 (1992) 19-44 "...there is a hidden fascination in this woman and her repulsive justice that we recognize with reluctance." (p. 39) .

Rehm, Rush "*Medea* and the *logos* of the heroic," *Eranos* 87 (1989) 97-115. "From the start, the play presents us with a woman alienated and victimized in a world controlled by men. We watch with sympathy and approval as she struggles to articulate a set of values different from those that entrap her, striving to break free from the *logos* of the male heroic. We are all the more disturbed when she finally gives into those values, for the results are catastrophic" (p. 114).

Visser, Margaret "Medea: daughter, sister, wife and mother. Natal family *versus* conjugal family in Greek and Roman myths about women," in M. Cropp et al., edd., *Greek Tragedy and its legacy. Essays presented to D. J. Conacher* (Calgary, l986) 149-65. "In Euripides' hands, *Medea* has become the negation of the ancient picture of marriage as it is drawn in a story like 'The Sabine Women'; instead of providing a fruitful and profitable link between two families, keeping a loving relationship alive in both households at once, Medea destroys first one family and then the other" (158-9).

Williamson, Margaret "A woman's place in Euripides' *Medea*," in Anton Powell ed., *Euripides, women, and sexuality* (London & N.Y., 1990) 16-31. "In marking that emergence [the emergence of Medea into view of the audience at line 214] so sharply by means of the linguistic and conceptual discontinuities and distortions which I have discussed, the play seems to me to be pointing, among other things, to the inadequacy of the language available for thinking about the *oikos* [household]. The private, it suggests by analogy, cannot be spoken in the language of the public except on condition of its destruction; and Medea's status as representative of the private was compromised as soon as she emerged into public view" (p.27).

Additional Bibliographical Note (2005)

A new edition by Donald Mastronarde with commentary, very full introductory material and extensive bibliography appeared in 2002 (Cambridge Univ. Press). On a smaller scale and for a somewhat different audience is a volume in the series Duckworth Companions to Greek and Roman Tragedy, *Euripides: Medea* by William Allan (London: Duckworth, 2002). He analyzes the play section-by-section and in subsequent chapters takes up individual topics: "Husbands and Wives" (male vs. female in the play); "Greeks and Others" (Medea's foreignness); "Medea's Revenge" (the horror, but in this play almost the necessity of matricide); and "Multi-Medea" (selected retellings of Medea's story in later literature, drama and film; see also *Medea in performance 1500-2000* below).

Several collections of essays have appeared:

Médée et la Violence, vol 45 (1996) of the journal *Pallas*, published at the University of Toulouse, includes articles by C. Segal (M. typifies the reversal in the realm of gender and in the moral and civic order, which is male-dominated), V. Citti (*Medea* fits Goethe's conception of tragedy as grounded in an irreconcilable opposition, and is in that sense "modern"), A. Mellero Bellido (other Medeas in fifth-century drama, especially satyr play), D. Pralon (M. in Euripides's *Peliades*), F. Jouan (all the characters come to recognize M.'s fearful power, some sooner, others - like Jason - too late), M. Menu (M. annihilates what she has - her children - to become what she truly is, granddaughter of the Sun), H. Sztulman (the psychopathology of M. as an early serial killer), J.-A. López Férez (the *sophia*-theme in the play), M. Fartzoff (M. exercises a quasi-"tyrannical" power to assert her own autonomy), L. Bordaux (traditional stage devices are used to show M.'s ascendancy over her enemies in a spectacular and pathetic way), A. Arcellaschi (violence in Seneca's *Medea*), M.-H. Garelli-François (M.'s role reverses that of the mourning mothers in Seneca's *Trojan Women*), H. Guiraud (M. on fifth- and fourth-century French drama), J.-C. Ranger (M. as a figure of violence in Euripides and later drama). D.-N. Mimoso-Ruiz (M. as representing "aesthetic" violence in art of the nineteenth and cinema of the twentieth centuries).

Medea: Essays on Medea in myth, literature, philosophy and art, edited by J.J. Clauss and S.I. Johnston (Princeton: Princeton Univ. Press, 1997): the development of the mythic tradition in various locales and in successive periods in relation to initiation rites (Fritz Graf); the myth as connected with rites of atonement and appeasement of a reproductive daimon that might otherwise harm young children and pregnant women (Sarah Iles Johnston); Medea as a "foundation-heroine" in Colchis, Cyrene and among the Medes (Nita Krevans); Medea killed her brother Apsyrtus to sever all connections with her family and natal home (Jan N. Bremmer); Medea's somewhat problematic appearance in Pindar's *Fourth Pythian Ode* (Dolores M. O'Higgins); Euripides gave a certain fixity to the previously shifting aspects of Medea's character (Deborah Boedeker); M.'s role as helper-maiden to the "hero" Jason in Bk. 3 of Apollonio's *Argonautika* (James J. Clauss); Ovid's reworking of the Medea story in *Met. 7* "into an open-ended form that offers divergent perspectives on the problems of marriage, betrayal, and power" (Carole E. Newlands, at p. 208); "Medea among the Philosophers", especially the Stoic philosopher Chrysippos's use of the myth (John M. Dillon); Medea as the snake/serpent in Seneca's *Medea* (Martha C. Nussbaum); Medea's shift from "normal" (that is, unthreatening) Greek woman in the body of Euripides's play to an "orientally" attired and therefore dangerous female "other" at the end (Christianne Sourvinou-Inwood); modern, especially twentieth-century, embodiments of Medea as a revolutionary symbol (Marianne McDonald).

Medea in performance 1500-2000, edited by Edith Hall, Fiona Macintosh and Oliver Taplin (Oxford: Legenda [European Humanities Research Centre], 2000). Medea in the English Renaissance (Diane Purkiss); on the 18th cent. London stage (Edith Hall) and the mid-Victorian stage (Fiona Macintosh); on film (Ian Christie) and in opera (Marianne McDonald); in Greece (Platon Mavromoustakos); central Europe (Eva Stehlíková); Japan (Mae Smethurst); in a Georgian adaptation (Olga Taxidou).

There have also appeared an assortment of relevant articles and book-chapters:

Beck, Jan-Wilhelm "Euripides' 'Medea': Dramatisches Vorbild oder misslungene Konzeption?," *Nachrichten der Akademie der Wissenschaften in Göttingen* I. philologisch-historische Klasse 1998 nr. 1 "[t]he story, just as depressing today as in the past, of a woman who by murdering her own children brings to fulfilment what is most unbelievable and most unnatural, who places her wish for revenge over her own most personal feelings as a mother" (5), has exercised a powerful impact on subsequent representations of the story. The author discusses many of these in detail and in a useful Appendix tabulates dramatic and operatic (including film and TV) versions pp. (35-41).

Burnett, Ann Pippin "Connubial revenge. Euripides' *Medea*," pp. 192-224 in Burnett, *Revenge in Attic and later tragedy* (Berkeley: Univ. of California Press, 1998) Medea "is a heroine exploited, like Clytemnestra, by extrahuman powers, but, unlike Agamemnon's queen, she is countercommanded by her insurgent female self, so that her finished deed demands horror and consternation from its audience, but strong pity as well for her who must accomplish it" (194).

Foley, Helene "Tragic wives: Medea's divided self", pp. 243-71 in Foley, *Female acts in Greek tragedy* (Princeton: Princeton Univ. Press, 2001). This is an updated version of Foley's essay in *Classical Antiquity* 8, 1989 (see p. 83 above).

Hall, Edith "Medea and British legislation before the First World War," *Greece and Rome* n.s. 46 (1999) 42-77. British audiences found the figure of mother-as-murderess so disturbing that, until the twentieth century, Euripides's play was performed mainly in toned-down adaptations and "did not become a standard part of the commercial repertoire until the relatively recent upsurge of feminism in the 1970s" (72).

Lawrence, Stuart "Audience uncertainty and Euripides' *Medea*," *Hermes* 125 (1997) 49-55. "Euripides [in the finale] undermines that holiest of polarized distinctions [the "gulf between mortals and gods"] by actually reifying in a visual metaphor the idea that a mortal may be 'demonic'" (55).

López Férez, Juan Antonio "Nueva lectura de *sophia-sophós* en la *Medea* de Eurípides," *EIKASMOS* 13 (2002) 41-61. "…Euripides is a poet interested in the linguistic usage of certain traditional words [like *sophia* and *sophos*], inherited from epic or lyric, attentive as he was in a special way to the new semantic values that some of the terms were acquiring in the Athens of his own day" (59).

McClure, Laura "'The Worst husband': discourses of praise and blame in Euripides' *Medea*," *Classical Philology* 94 (1999) 373-94. "Through Medea's abusive language, the play suggests a transgression of normative gender roles that prefigures her elevation to semi-divine status at the end of the play" (373).

Mueller, Melissa "The Language of reciprocity in Euripides' *Medea*," *American Journal of Philology* 122 (2001) 471-504. An important dynamic in the play is set up by the various relations that revolve about *charis* and *philia*, reciprocal gift-giving and indebtedness, and –of course– ultimately revenge.

Newman, J. Kevin "Euripides' *Medea*: structures of estrangement," *Illinois Classical Studies* 26 (2001) 53-76. Euripides's version uses various techniques of estrangement, *Entfremdung*, and presents M. as in part "a primitive dragon spirit who impinges on Greek rationality, estranging its sanitized world" (58).

Schmidt, Jens-Uwe "Der Kindermord der fremden Kolcherin - ein tragischer Konflikt? Überlegungen zur *Medea* des Euripides," *Rheinisches Museum für Philologie* n.f. 142 (1999) 243-72. "…the cause of the powerlessness [of Medea's reason] can only be sought in the orientation of the action according to heroic norms which demand of her that she subordinate even her love for her children and the center of her life which is grounded on that love to the greatness of her own esteem and recognition" (269).

Syropoulos, Spiridon D. "The Invention and use of the infanticide motif in Euripides' *Medea*," *Platon* 52 (2001-2002) 126-38. "[B]ecause what she did was an irreparable wrong, committed freely and consciously" Euripides deflects any initial sympathy for Medea and "makes sure that she remains forever stigmatized" (136-7).

Van Zyl Smit, Betine "Medea the feminist," *Acta Classica* 45 (2002) 101-22. This study of several modern re-workings of the myth (some quite radical) concludes by emphasizing "the important place Medea has taken in the minds of creative women" (120). The same author has also produced an unpublished dissertation, *Contemporary Witch: dramatic treatments of the Medea myth* (University of Stellenbosch, S. Africa, 1987).

Zerba, Michelle "Medea *hypokrites*," *Arethusa* 35 (2002) 315-37. "In no other extant tragedy are we made as aware as we are in the *Medea* of the actorly premise that underlies the conception of the chief agent, and in no other tragedy is the premise played out more brilliantly and sensationally" (327).